David R. B. Nevin

Continental Sketches of Distinguished Pennsylvanians

David R. B. Nevin

Continental Sketches of Distinguished Pennsylvanians

ISBN/EAN: 9783337009960

Printed in Europe, USA, Canada, Australia, Japan

Cover: Foto ©ninafisch / pixelio.de

More available books at **www.hansebooks.com**

CONTINENTAL

SKETCHES

OF

DISTINGUISHED PENNSYLVANIANS.

BY
DAVID R. B. NEVIN.

WITH AN APPENDIX,

CONTAINING IMPORTANT STATE PAPERS,
AND VALUABLE STATISTICAL AND HISTORICAL INFORMATION,
SELECTED FROM AUTHENTIC SOURCES.

PHILADELPHIA:
PORTER & COATES, 822 CHESTNUT STREET.
1875.

PREFATORY.

O N the threshold of our Centennial festivities
while the air is redolent with the rich aroma
of cherished memories and pure resolves, we proffer
no apology for giving to the world brief but truthful
sketches of distinguished Pennsylvanians, whose
wisdom in council, and valor in battle, contributed
so much to the triumph of the national arms, in the
grand old days of the Revolution. The galaxy of
greatness developed in that historic period borrowed
much of its splendor from our own local firmament,
and the names of Franklin, Wayne, and Morris,
stanch exponents of philosophy, valor, and finance,
have always been recognized as among its brightest
stars. A plain, unadorned recital of the virtues of
such an ancestry cannot fail to impart a useful moral,
and stimulate a noble ambition to emulate those
heroic traits of which they were the bold, expressive
type. Aside from our natural personal obligations
to cherish their memories on the basis of gratitude
and consanguinity, a closer scrutiny of their motives,

and a more acute analysis of their actions, cannot
fail to elicit our most enthusiastic commendation.
Amid a cloudy atmosphere of doubt and danger,
they exhibited a blended patience and fortitude almost peerless in the annals of history. Their military prowess seemed whetted by adversity, and the
bright sunshine of long delayed victory culminated
in the development of a profound and exalted statesmanship.

The spirit that animated, and the ambition that
spurred them, were neither restricted nor central-
ized, but as limitless and elastic as the mountain air,
permeating the length and breadth of their colonial
area, flourishing as generously amid the hills and
glens of the interior as beneath the sacred shadows
of Independence Hall in their own loyal metropolis.
There was a simplicity, purity, dignity, and positive
culture, about these colonial heroes worthy our strictest emulation, and the life of each was a compendium of penury, peril, and heroic sacrifice; his material and moral victories being achieved on battle
fields well studded with monuments of private grief
and personal ruin. The primitive legislation of colonial Pennsylvania, though eminently cautious and
conservative, was firm and prudent. It was not of
the Vesuvian order, belching forth an indiscriminate

volume of patriotic lava; but, like the waters of her own majestic Delaware, its fountains were pure, its channels deep, and its progress irresistible. Its clear, straight, manly denunciation of Ministerial despotism was only awarded when public wrongs or private grievances were clearly ascertained and distinctly specified. That cautious legislation which at the incipiency of the Revolution was condemned by many as too tardy for an imminent crisis, asserted itself at the proper time in a proud and lofty vindication of colonial honor, and a happy avoidance of flagrant blunders, humiliating rescindings, and unmanly compromises. Our general government has passed through the Revolutionary, the Confederate, and the Constitutional forms. The first extended from the meeting of the *first* Continental Congress, March 5, 1774, to the final ratification of the Articles of Confederation, March 1, 1781.

The second extended from the ratification of the Articles of Confederation, to the time the Constitution went into operation, March 4, 1789.

The third is that form which has existed from the latter period to the present time.

The Revolutionary and Confederate forms, extending from 1774 to 1789, were eminently fruitful in the production of great men, and to that period we will more particularly, though not exclusively, confine our selections.

Their lives have survived the criticisms of a century, their memories are deeply imbedded in the national heart, and a reproduction of their virtues we trust will be acceptable to their worthy descendants throughout the stanch old Commonwealth for which they did so much.

For the historical and statistical matter contained in the Appendix, we acknowledge our indebtedness, to, more particularly, Hazard's Archives of Pennsylvania, the American Archives, Hazard's Register and Proud's History of Pennsylvania.

Continental Sketches.

ROBERT MORRIS, OF PHIL'A.

Incidents and Developments in the life of the Great Financier of the Revolution—From the school to the counting-house—Schemes and theories conceived and executed with wonderful celerity and dash—The deliberate but cheerful sacrifice when the crisis in our history came—A hard knot untied.

THE great financier of the Revolution, who undoubtedly contributed more to its successful termination than any civilian of that historic period, was a lifelong resident, but not a native, of Philadelphia. Robert Morris was born in Lancashire, England, in 1733, and removed to this country at the early age of thirteen. His father was a Liverpool merchant, largely engaged in the American trade, a gentleman of strict integrity, and active, progressive business habits and tastes. The captain of a vessel consigned to him, on its arrival fired what was intended as a complimentary salute to Mr. Morris, but the gun-wad unfortunately struck that gentleman, producing so serious a wound as to terminate his life in a few days thereafter. Young Morris, immediately on his arrival here, was placed at one of the best schools in Philadelphia, but, for some inexplicable reason, his scholastic career was not remarkable. At fifteen he was withdrawn from academic walls and inducted into the commercial office of Mr. Charles Willing, at that time one of the leading merchants of Philadelphia. He served what was then termed a regular apprenticeship with that gentleman for two years—for in those days commercial as well as literary educations were more thorough and complete than now, and only attainable by much labor and system. Ready-made merchants were as rarely heard of at that time as ready-made lawyers, and the solid foundations thus cautiously prepared were generally surmounted by worthy and honorable superstructures. Mr. Morris had the advantage of superior culture and training, for his preceptor, Charles Willing, as we have intimated, was an honor to the mercantile profession, and remarkable for the scope, vigor, and forecast of his understanding, his great executive ability, unblemished integrity, and the amenity of his disposition and manners. In such a school, with such an instructor, the young commercial aspirant made great headway, and in a few years formed intimate business relations with Mr. Thomas Willing, the son of his esteemed patron, and for forty years the old firm of Willing & Morris was recognized in commercial circles as one of the most trustworthy and reliable in the city of Philadelphia. This firm was amicably dissolved in 1793, and Thomas Willing, the senior member, a high-toned, christian gentleman, died in 1821, aged 89 years. Bereft of parental counsel, the early life of Mr. Morris makes a glowing exhibit of fidelity, executive ability, self-reliance, and expansive ideas. His whole life, from early childhood to venerable old age, is dotted with incidents and developments indicating great breadth of thought in everything pertaining to finance. Schemes and theories of his, before which the ordinary mind would quail with nervous fear, were conceived and executed by him with wonderful celerity and dash, sometimes evoking from him heavy personal sacrifices to carry his point. Some minds have a sufficiency of nerve and daring to attempt the tunneling of the Andes, whilst others, cast in a more cautious mould, shrink from the perforation of a molehill.

Robert Morris watched with an intelligent and anxious eye the encroachments of the British government upon the liberties of his countrymen, and, although his private interests might suffer, he never shrank from honest protest and vigorous action in her defence, when duty made the demand. His firm was the largest importing one, perhaps, in Philadelphia; yet in 1765, when the crisis seemed to render it necessary, he cheerfully signed the non-importation agreement entered into by his fellow-merchants, although he sustained very heavy private losses by the act. The sacrifice was a deliberate but cheerful one; yet he allowed no selfish consideration to

1*·

clog the path of honorable duty. There is a moral grandeur in the performance of any conscientious duty, doubly itensified when the act conflicts with private interests, draining your depleted treasury, and severing perhaps the friendships of a lifetime.

The battle of Lexington was fought April, 1775, and the news reached Philadelphia in *four* days, which at that time was considered a remarkably speedy transmittal. It produced a thrilling sensation throughout the whole land, particularly in Philadelphia. Mr. Morris, when the news reached the city, was one of a large number of gentlemen assembled at the famous old "City Tavern" to celebrate St. George's day. Immediately after the reception of the news the groaning, hospitable tables were all deserted, and the patron saint was soon forgotten in the eager and restless anxiety to hear the news from Lexington. From that moment Mr. Morris was in favor of a quick and final separation from the mother country, and, during the balance of his life did all he could to effect that object. On the 3d of November, 1775, he was elected by the Legislature of Pennsylvania a delegate to the second Congress that met in Philadelphia. A short time thereafter he was appointed on a secret committee authorized by the preceding Congress, whose duty it was "to contract for the importation of arms, ammunition, sulphur and saltpetre, and to export produce on the public account to pay for the same." His recognized business capacity, the celerity of his actions, and his almost inexhaustible creative power, made his presence indispensable on all important committees where finance and revenue were considered. He was well and favorably acquainted with every business man and firm in Philadelphia, and availed himself of this fact to borrow money on his own personal responsibility whenever the stringent exigencies of the Government required assistance. This he did very frequently, and was always prompt and punctual in the re-payment of all personal loans thus negotiated. When Congress, in December, 1776, was unfortunately compelled to retire from Philadelphia, owing to the approach of the British army, Mr. Morris was one of a committee of three detailed to remain and transact all Continental business. While engaged in this sphere, he received a sad letter from General Washington, in which he gave a vivid description of the lamentable condition of the army, on account of their not being paid. Our forces were at that time located on the Delaware river, opposite Trenton. The General was anxious to make an offensive demonstration, and to do this required ten thousand dollars. He looked anxiously for relief to Mr. Morris as his last and only hope. He had made several similar applications to other parties, but in each instance had been disappointed. Mr. Morris, with deep feeling and emotion, read and re-read the letter from his beloved chieftain, but what to do he knew not. The sum desired, it was true, was small, but his own private exchequer was exhausted and demoralized, and the men of means (and they were comparatively few in those days) had left the city. He pondered over the letter in his counting-room until weary, not knowing what to do or where to go for this comparatively trifling and yet essentially necessary sum. On his way home he met an old Quaker, with whom he had but a slight acquaint-ance, and who, in addition, was a practical, conscien-tious Peace man, opposed to all wars except against Satan, and that he desired to prosecute with nervous vigor. This was a hard knot to untie, but Morris, who had great tact and magnetic conversational powers attempted the discouraging task. To the inquiry of the Quaker as to the news of the day, Morris replied that he had but little, and that was very depressing. He then, in his own enthusiastic and attractive way, told him all the facts, and closed by showing him the autograph letter of Washington, and explaining the almost vital necessity of having ten thousand dollars at once. The honest Quaker faltered but a moment under fire of such guns, and replied composedly, " *Friend Robert, thou shall have it.*" In one hour the money was transmitted to Washington's headquarters, and was indirectly in-strumental, under Providence, in gaining a signal victory over the Hessians at Trenton, thus changing the whole current of the war, animating the droop-ing spirits of the tattered, hungry, and penniless patriots, and correspondingly depressing the proud hopes and predictions of the arrogant foe.

In 1779 the army was alarmingly destitute of all sorts of military stores and supplies, particularly lead. Old clock-weights, and all similar articles that could possibly be used for the purpose, were melted down for army use, but the supply could not be kept up in this crude and irregular way, and the crisis was becoming serious and startling. At this critical juncture one of Mr. Morris' privateers fortunately arrived with a cargo of ninety tons of lead, one-half of which belonging to him personally he immediately forwarded to the army, and two days thereafter bought the balance with his own private means, and shipped it on the same patriotic errand. We might multiply instances of the genuine liberality and opportune tact of this great man, but will refer to but one more, which cannot be repeated too often, and which is eminently worthy the admiration and gratitude of every American citizen.

In 1781 General Washington contemplated the capture of New York city. This was in accordance with an understanding between him and Count Rochambeau, and it was arranged that the French fleet under De Barras and De Grasse should co-operate with our land forces to secure the desired result. On the arrival of the fleet the whole plan was frustrated by the announcement of the Admiral that he would not enter the bay of New York, but would harbor for a few weeks in Chesapeake Bay. The reduction of New York was not only rendered impracticable, but actually impossible. It is very re-

liable history that at this very critical moment
Robert Morris, of Philadelphia, suggested quietly to
the commanding general the propriety of immediately attacking Cornwallis in the South. It is also
well known that this was the most brilliant military
move of the campaign, and practically ended the
whole war. However historiographers may differ as
to the creative mind that developed this move, they
cannot differ as to where the funds came from to
prosecute that particular part of the campaign.

Nearly every dollar and every war supply of that
memorable campaign was a generous personal advance based on the individual credit of Robert Morris. He furnished the army of General Washington, at a time when victory was not by any means
an assured fact, and the loan therefore proportion-
ately more risky, with eighty siege guns, one hundred pieces of field artillery, with all necessary ammunition and other appurtenances, and within thirty
days from his original interview with Washington
all these supplies and artillery were in possession of
the latter. This was astounding; but the whole
has not been told. The entire army at this time
was fed, clothed, and paid solely on the personal
credit of this same Robert Morris, who actually issued his own promissory notes for the enormous
sum of one million four hundred thousand dollars,
every dime of which was promptly paid by him at
maturity. All this was done without the slightest

hope of profit or plunder, for the integrity of the great financier was above all suspicion.

In 1781 he was unanimously appointed what was termed Superintendent of Finance. The duties of this office were multifarious and onerous, and, we may add, thankless. He had to examine the state of the public debt, expenditures and revenue, digest and report plans for improving and regulating the finances, and had also sole control of the management and disbursement of all the foreign loans, national and individual, in France and Holland, public funds of every possible character, and the disbursement of the same for the support of every branch of the Government, military, naval, and civil—in brief, all the moneyed operations of the country were under his control, and this, too, at a time when great distress prevailed in every section of the land, and public credit was a shattered wreck. The Treasury was two and a half millions in arrears, the creditors generally being illiberal and grasping, and unwilling to compromise for aught but cash. The paper bills of credit, floating loosely and promiscuously around the country, were almost entirely valueless, and soldier and citizen jointly suffered in the midst of this alarming distress. All this time the private notes of Morris were worth "their face," and constituted the principal medium for all large transactions. He worked with a will in his official position to bring public confidence to a wholesome standard, and gradually succeeded in bringing order, system and symmetry out of distrust, demoralization and chaos. He established the old Bank of North America, which was eminently instrumental in restoring public credit, encouraging public improvements, and · producing general and unbounded public confidence, the true panacea of all financial crises.

Though many financiers may have had more brilliant administrations, producing, perhaps, more voluminous results, receiving the praise of servile dependents, echoed by a subsidized and partisan press, we fail to find, in the history of this country at least, a financier of such creative genius, bold design, and fearless execution, as Robert Morris of Pennsylvania. His Congressional career, like his private character, was "without spot or blemish." Whatever he did was always well done; and as Colonial legislator, member of Congress and of the Constitutional Convention, no one ever exhibited more zeal and sacrificed more comfort and ease for the good of his country and his fellow-men. An unfortunate land speculation, however, shattered his private fortune in his latter days, and the brilliant financier of Colonial and Revolutionary times was in his old days reduced to comparative poverty. Amidst all these severe trials and afflictions, he always asserted his inherent manhood by a calm, dignified, and philosophic demeanor. Worn down with public labor and private misfortune, he died, May 8, 1806, aged 73 years.

BENJAMIN RUSH, OF PHILADELPHIA.

His early studies at a Maryland Academy, Princeton College, and Edinburgh University—Professor in the First Medical School ever organized in the United States—The Onslaught by Journalists, Pamphleteers, and anonymous writers during the reign of the yellow fever in 1793, &c.

IN the old township of Byberry, some fourteen miles northeast of Philadelphia, Dr. Benjamin Rush was born on the 24th of December, 1745, his ancestors having emigrated from England to that section of Pennsylvania about the year 1683. His father dying when he was six years old, his mother, a most estimable lady, with a keen appreciation of the inestimable advantages of a good education, determined to give her son the very best opportunity for its acquisition her limited means would allow. He was accordingly sent to a somewhat celebrated academy located at Nottingham, Md., at that time under the control and management of the venerable Rev. Dr. Finley, a ripe scholar and cultivated gentleman, subsequently president of Princeton College. The residents of that section of Maryland were remarkable for their honest simplicity and correct morality, and this fact, coupled with the literary

tastes and solid merits of his pious and learned preceptor, contributed no little to the formation of his
early acquired good character. After a residence
here of five years, where his moral qualities were
always abreast of his classical attainments, he entered
Princeton College, as an advanced student, in 1759.
Such was the completeness of his preparatory course
at Nottingham, that, although the youngest student
in his class, in fact, a mere boy, he was the peer of
any of his fellows in all his collegiate studies. He
received his degree of A. B. in 1760, before he had
reached his fifteenth year, perhaps the youngest
graduate before or since of his venerable Alma
Mater. Soon after the completion of his collegiate
course he enrolled himself as a student in the medical office of the eminent Dr. Redman, of Philadelphia, and was one of Dr. Shippen's ten pupils
who attended the first course of anatomical lectures
ever given in this country. Gifted with an investi-
gating mind he studied closely and assiduously, with
a determination to learn, and in 1766 sailed for
Edinburgh, where he resumed his studies for two
years, receiving at the end of that time, 1768, his
degree of M. D. from the University there. After
spending a year in Continental travel, mingling with
the most cultivated medical men in London and
Paris, he returned to his native country and commenced the practice of medicine in Philadelphia.
At the very early age of twenty-four he was elected
professor of chemistry in the college of Philadelphia,

and became, about the same time, a popular contributor to medical and general literature, his foreign residence and unwearied industry having materially enlarged his professional views and attainments. The present University of Pennsylvania was at that time in creative process, Drs. Shippen, Ruhn, Bond, and Morgan, having for a year or two been delivering lectures at irregular and uncertain intervals. The acquisition of young Rush completed the corps of professors of the first medical school ever organized in the United States. Some fifteen years thereafter the primitive institution referred to was merged in the present University, and Dr. Rush, then recognized as one of the brilliant young physicians of the country, held the position of professor of the institutes and practice, also of clinical practice, in the new combination which for almost a century has wielded such a power in medical circles, and quietly earned such an honorable reputation. Without possessing any very marked oratorical powers, Dr. Rush was an interesting and popular lecturer. His language was simple and always intelligible, his scientific disquisitions profound, without being drowsy and heavy, and his lectures abounded with pleasant and pointed anecdotes, and occasional brilliant sallies of a somewhat poetic imagination.

He was an eminently minute man, garnering carefully every floating fact, theory, and incident, and treasuring them carefully for future utilization; absorbing everything, forgetting nothing.

In 1790, after a successful professional experience of twenty years, he gave to the public, in book form, his new principles of medicine. His views were confronted by strong opposition at the time of their promulgation. He had great confidence in a free use of the lancet, and abiding faith in the power and utility of calomel, which he styled " the Samson of the Materia Medica." His opponents yielded to the Samsonian illustration, because, as they jocosely re-remarked, "it has slain its thousands." Modern science, although not entirely abandoning, has very greatly modified the use of these potential agencies, for which Dr. Rush so ably contended, and which, under his skillful control, were productive of such beneficent results.

In 1793, Philadelphia was terribly scourged with the yellow fever. The city had been free from it for thirty-one years, but now it assumed the shape of a fearful epidemic, and swept over the town with the horrible celerity of a prairie fire, destroying everything it touched. It thus raged from July to November, averaging forty deaths daily, and aggregating some five thousand victims, a heavy proportion considering the population of Philadelphia at that time. The whole city was panic-stricken, for the swift-winged messenger of death baffled all professional skill to subdue it, and the great metropolis was being rapidly transformed into a huge charnel house. During this fearful crisis Dr. Rush was making herculean efforts to subdue the deadly foe, work-

ing with a will during part of his time, and appropriating the balance to a thorough analysis of the
desease from a scientific standpoint. He visited over
one hundred and fifty patients a week, and saved
many thousand lives by his original and judicious
treatment. His special mode of treatment, successful as it was, was severely criticised by many distinguished medical contemporaries and was productive of great prejudice against him. Journalists,
pamphleteers, and scurrilous anonymous writers
hurled their fierce javelins at him with reckless
malignity, until the discussion, originally based on
questions of professional skill, degenerated into a
petty, personal persecution. He was even stigmatized as a murderer, and threatened with mobocratic
expulsion from his native city. In this instance
public sentiment assumed one of those peculiar roles
not uncommon in history, invariably as unjust as
they are inexplicable.

As a penalty for his blood-circulation theory
Harvey blunted his professional prospects, and was
hooted as a common fool; and Dr. Rush, by his brilliant practice, productive of the most successful results in saving human life, lost public confidence
because he bravely wandered from the beaten path
of official routine to subdue a pestilential foe which,
until then, had never been vanquished. On the termination of the fever a motion was made in a public meeting of the citizens to cordially thank the
medical faculty of Philadelphia generally, and Dr.

Benjamin Rush specially, for their eminent services during the epidemic, but no one in the vast audience was bold enough to second it, and it failed. The noble survivors were grateful to Providence . and their own strong constitutions for the general result, but were cautious about taking any additional stock in the medical fraternity. Phil Frenan, the dashing, reckless editor of the New York *Advertiser*, who had acquired a national reputation by his pungent paragraphs and satirical verses, complained that the physicians had fled the city:

> On prancing steed, with sponge at nose,
>   From town behold Sangrado fly;
> Camphor and tar, where'er he goes,
>   The infected shafts of death defy—
> Safe in an atmosphere of scents
> He leaves us to our own defence.

William Cobbett, an intelligent Englishman, residing in Philadelphia at the time, a popular political pamphleteer, flying the original *nom de plume* of "Peter Porcupine," was a man of bitter force and strength, and a consummate master of invective. He violently attacked Rush in one of his publications, and was sued by the latter for libel, and made to pay $5,000 for his sport. This was one of the many assaults made upon Dr. Rush, but he survived them all, and built up and retained by all odds the largest practice in Philadelphia. A few years afterwards there was a re-actionary feeling in his favor by his receiving from the King of Prussia, in 1805, a gold medal for his replies to certain questions about the treatment of yellow fever. For the same consideration he received, in 1807, a medal from the Queen of Etruria, and in 1811 the Emperor of Russia gave him a brilliant diamond ring, through respect for his great medical fame.

Dr. Rush was a voluminous and able writer, and one wonders how he could spare so much time from his laborious professional duties to assume the role of an essayist and a general writer on literary, moral, philosophical, and political subjects. One solution is that he was a most zealous, indefatigable worker, allowing no small fragments of time to be wasted. His writings consist principally of seven volumes, six of which are devoted to medical subjects, the remaining one being a compendium of various literary articles. His " Medical Inquiries and Observations," "Diseases of the Mind," " Medical Tracts," "Health, Temperance, and Exercise," gave him a deservedly high reputation at home, and honorable recognition abroad.

In the early part of his life Dr. Rush found sufficient leisure time to study politics, not with the circumscribed instincts of a selfish, sordid partisan, but as a good citizen, with an honest desire to assist in shaping the political destinies of his country. In 1776 he was a member of the celebrated Congress that gave us an historic Declaration of Independence, to which he cheerfully and proudly gave his name and influence. In 1777 he was appointed physician-general of the military hospital in the

Middle Department, and in 1787 was a member of the Pennsylvania Convention which ratified the Federal Constitution, but was not a member of the General Constitutional Convention, as has been erroneously stated by some authorities. He did all he could do for its adoption, considering it "a masterpiece of human wisdom.". In 1799, President Adams appointed him Treasurer of the United States Mint, solely on account of his faultless character and sterling integrity, and which was entirely unsolicited on his part. The duties of this office he faithfully performed during the last fourteen years of his life. But few cities in Europe, and certainly none in this country, have such numerous and various charitable institutions as Philadelphia. No one citizen contributed more to the successful organization of many of these than Dr. Benjamin Rush. In 1785, he planned and organized the Philadelphia Dispensary, the first institution of the kind in the country. He was president of the Philadelphia Society for the Abolition of Slavery, and also of the Philadelphia Medical Society. He was the founder of the Philadelphia Bible Society, and for many years one of its honored presiding officers, and for several years was vice president of the celebrated American Philosophical Society. He was a strong, practical friend of the temperance cause, and his work entitled "An Inquiry into the Effect of Ardent Spirits upon the Human Body and Mind" is full of valuable information, and is considered standard authority among the friends of this particular reformatory movement. He presented a thousand copies of this interesting tract to the General Assembly of the Presbyterian Church for general distribution among their members, evoking from them at the time a stronger resolution in favor of temperance than they have ever promulgated since. Dr. Rush was a public writer for forty-nine years, and was not a mere collator of other men's opinions, but an original, honest searcher after truth, combining utility and elegance in all his essays on physical science or polite literature. He was, moreover, a high-toned, Christian gentleman, and the sneers and fascinations of what are termed fashionable circles were powerless to divert him from the path of honest and honorable rectitude. His private life was one of unsullied purity, and his public career is unsurpassed for its many brilliant developments and practical results for the common good of his country and his fellow men.

BENJAMIN FRANKLIN, PRINTER.

The man in whose honor the Franklin Institute was named—A Boston and Philadelphia Statesman—The central figure of our local Continental worthies—A home portrait of the Editor-Statesman of 1776.

THE Pennsylvania signers to the Declaration of Independence were Robert Morris, Benjamin Rush, Benjamin Franklin, John Morton, George Clymer, James Smith, George Taylor, James Wilson, and George Ross. The signers to the Constitution were Benjamin Franklin, Robert Morris, Thomas Fitzsimmons, James Wilson, Thomas Mifflin, George Clymer, Jared Ingersoll, and Gouverneur Morris. It will be observed that several of the original signers of the Declaration were leading members of the Constitutional Convention, and remembered that a majority of them were active participants in our Continental Congress. The average intellectuality of the convention was high, and, happily, very equally distributed, so far as latitude was concerned. Even in those primitive times there was considerable sectional feeling, and it required consummate tact and diplomacy to reconcile and harmonize these antagonisms. The Cavaliers of the South, as they

were pleased to term themselves, were nobly represented by Washington, "President and deputy from
Virginia," Jas. Madison, from the same State, Rutledge, the two Pinckneys, and Pierce Butler, of
South Carolina. The focus of New England's admiration was old Roger Sherman, a severe Puritan and an ardent patriot. New York was justly
proud of the youthful, *petite*, but graceful and eloquent, Alexander Hamilton, while Pennsylvania's
grand central figure was the grave and thoughtful
old Ben Franklin. Indeed, as diplomat, scientist,
philosopher, and patriot, he was a sort of *paterfa-
milias* in the grand group of national celebrities.
No shafts of envy were hurled at the veteran statesman, then in his eighty-first year; but his suggestions, theories, and opinions, had a wonderful influence on his fellow-members. To sketch the civil
heroes of our Colonial and Continental history, and
make no mention of Franklin, even on the hypoth-
esis that everybody knows all about him, would be
a flagrant and palpable omission of *Hamlet* in the
play. Although his name is a household word and
his fame historically grand, it is a singular fact that
no complete popular biography of this great man
has ever been published. One rarely meets with
his autobiography, save on the dusty shelves of
some second-hand book store; and Sparks' Life of
Franklin is too voluminous and heavy for general
currency and utility. As if to fill the vacancy, a
compact three-volume Life of Franklin is, at the

present writing, being issued from the press, edited by the Hon. John Bigelow, ex-minister to France. Franklin was perhaps the best specimen, of what is usually termed a self-made man, ever produced in this country. Men of this class are generally strong, but superficial, too often lacking culture and finish; but he was just the reverse of this, profound in learning, with the natural simplicity of a little child, and possessed of highly polished personal manners. Franklin was a remarkably handsome man, with a commanding figure above the middle size, and was in his early days, quite an athlete, and famous for his physical strength and activity. His countenance indicated self-poise and serenity, great depth of thought, and inflexible resolution. He possessed captivating conversational powers, and could adapt these very felicitously to circumstances, either in the laboratory of the scientist or at the desk of a school boy. Although a philosopher, he was something of a wag, and brimful of quaint good humor. When John Hancock appended his signature to the Declaration of Independence, in large, bold characters, he remarked with an air of excusable *bravado*, "There! John Bull can read *my* name without spectacles." A moment after, he turned to Franklin, and somewhat nervously suggested, "We must all hang together now." "Yes," responded the resolute old philosopher, "or most assuredly we will all hang separately," which was a good joke, and very true at the same time.

Born in Boston, January 17, 1706, it is not surprising that at an early age he soon wearied of the respectable, but not very intellectual, avocation of soap-boiler and chandler, a sphere which his practical father had selected for him. In 1722 he landed in Philadelphia, being at that time but a mere boy. From that date until his death, April 17, 1790, he was most thoroughly identified with all the important interests and developments of his adopted State, and, solely through intrinsic merit, was the recipient from her of many civil and political honors. He was made successively Clerk of the Assembly (1736), Postmaster of Philadelphia (1737), and Deputy Postmaster General for the British Colonies (1753). No young man in these days of zealous effort to win fame by short cuts and air-line routes, can fail to obtain much valuable information by studying closely the salient points in the character of this most remarkable man. Although a century has elapsed since he has passed away, an intelligent posterity cannot fail to mark the admirable and exquisitely adjusted features of his character, and the harmonious and massive grandeur of his magnificent and finely-developed manhood. Penniless and footsore, at sixteen years of age he entered our city, and in a few brief years (1752), without any of the modern manipulation and lobbying for titular distinction, the Royal Society of London unanimously elected him a member of their dignified body, and bestowed upon him the Copley gold medal for his brilliant discovery of the identity of lightning with the electric fluid. In the interim of these eventful years, his failures and successes, his defeats and triumphs, form a consolidated volume of profound interest, more thrilling than the most popular romance of modern times. Whether you view him as editor of the *Pennsylvania Gazette* and "Poor Richard's Almanac;" as mediator between the Assembly and the proprietary governments, compromising difficulties between them about taxation before the Privy Council of England; or, before the House of Commons, endeavoring to repeal the odious Stamp Act; . or, again, as ambassador at the court of France, adroitly securing the memorable treaty of alliance between that country and our own, so immensely favorable to us; in all these varied spheres of poverty, honor and trust, we find astounding developments of individuality and wisdom. Franklin's ancestral tree was not one of hot-house culture. His father was a plain, practical, poor man, from Northampton, England, a strict Puritan, and left his native soil during the reign of Charles II. to avoid the persecution raging there with fanatical zeal. He settled in Boston, and married a lady of respectable family in that city. The parents determined to make a clergyman of Benjamin, *nolens volens;* but slender resources, and, perhaps, lack of theological taste in the young man, changed their views, and he was withdrawn to assist his father in his business of tallow chandler. He soon became tired of this, for the business itself was not a congenial one, and, restless and uneasy, he longed for the deep blue sea—that El - Dorado of so many romantic youths of fifteen who become tired of the despotism of home rule. Then he became taciturn and thoughtful, developing a wonderful taste for reading, devouring everything within his reach, "Plutarch's Lives," "Defoe's Essay on Projects," and everything else in his father's scanty library. At twelve we find him at the printer's desk; at fourteen, proficient in the mechanical part of his trade, and zealously perfecting himself in prose composition. With great taste for learning, he imbibed a kindred one for disputation, and adopting the Socratic method, he became dextrous in confuting and confounding an antagonist by a series of questions. In early life he was somewhat skeptical in religious matters, and propagated his peculiar tenets with more zeal, perhaps, than judgment, until he found he did much injury to his companions by this course, when he very prudently desisted. In his maturer years, however, according to his warm, personal friend, Dr. William Smith, he became a believer in Divine revelation. In his "Memoirs," written by himself, he says: "'And here let me, with all humility, acknowledge that to Divine Providence I am indebted for all the happiness I have hitherto enjoyed. It is that power alone which has furnished me with the means I have employed and that has crowned them with success. My faith in this respect leads me to hope that the Divine goodness will still be exercised towards me. My future fortune is unknown but to Him whose hand is our destiny."

In this connection we insert the quaint epitaph written by himself long before his death :—

The body of
BENJAMIN FRANKLIN, PRINTER,
Like the cover of an old book,
Its contents torn out
And stript of its lettering and gilding,
Lies here, food for worms.
Yet the book itself shall not be lost,
For it will (as he believed) appear once more,
in a new
and more beautiful edition,
corrected and amended
by the Author.

The early life of Franklin, as we have seen, was obscured by dark clouds, and his pathway full of thorns. His parents were poor, and his father more particularly, unappreciative and unsympathetic; his brother, to whom he was indentured as a printer's apprentice, harsh, parsimonious, and despotic; his own means limited, and his health delicate. This was the atmosphere surrounding him, when at sixteen he sailed from Boston for New York, and failing to secure employment there, walked from the latter city to Philadelphia. On his arrival he had not a farthing, no counsellor, no acquaintance, no friend; he had to start from the crude surface and build up. He wandered through our long, narrow streets, not a pauper, but a delicate, penniless youth, but one within whose bosom was a riveted determination to work and win. Space will not permit us to enter into minute details of his career during the first few years of his life in Philadelphia. Sir William Keith, Governor of the Province, took stock in the young printer, and suggested the propriety of his going to England to purchase printing material and supplies to start his new paper in Philadelphia. He sailed for London, and when he arrived there found that Sir William, upon whose letters of credit he had relied, had deceived him, and he was compelled to search for something to do to support himself in that mammoth city. In 1726 he returned to Philadelphia and started his paper. In 1730 he married, and in 1732 began the publication of "Poor Richard's Almanac," which was continued for twenty-five years—a most valuable compendium of prudential maxims and sound common-sense, a republication of which might furnish useful reading, during the long winter nights, for our National and State legislators. Franklin's political career commenced in 1736, and during the same year he assisted in the establishment of the American Philosophical Society and the University of Pennsylvania. In 1738 he formed the first fire company ever organized in Philadelphia, to which was shortly afterward added an insurance office against losses by fire. In 1742 he published his celebrated treatise upon the improvement of chimneys, following this by inventing a stove known as the "Franklin," used for a century

2*

in all parts of the country. In the French war of
1744 he proposed a plan of voluntary association
for the defence of the country, which was joined by
ten thousand persons, trained to the use and exercise of arms. He was chosen colonel of the Philadelphia regiment, but declined the honor in favor of
a friend. The same year he was elected a member
of the Provincial Assembly, where he remained for
ten years. He now devoted his time more particularly to philosophical and scientific researches, and
in 1752 fixed an insulated iron rod to his own residence to protect it from lightning, for which act his
profound and wise neighbors deemed him a fit subject for a lunatic asylum. In 1753 he assumed the
office of Deputy Postmaster General of America, and,
strange as it may seem to our modern postal officials,
he made the Post Office Department a source of
revenue to the British Crown, instead of a tax upon
the people for its support. At this period Braddock was defeated in his wild and reckless expedition against Fort Du Quesne, and the whole frontier
was exposed to the incursions of the savages and the
French. Franklin dropped his philosophy and his
metaphysics, and at the head of a company of bold
volunteers marched to the protection of our frontier.
In 1757 the militia were disbanded by order of the
British government, shortly after which Franklin
was appointed agent to adjust the difficulties which
had arisen between the citizens of Pennsylvania and
the proprietary government. He sailed for Europe

to lay the matter before the Privy Council. His fame as a philosopher had preceded him, and unsought on his part he received honorable degrees at London, Edinburgh, and Oxford. In 1764 he again returned to England to settle if possible the stamp-act difficulty, and lay the facts before the Crown. In 1766 and 1767 he made a trip to Holland, Germany, and France, where he met with most flattering and distinguished receptions. His subsequent connection with the celebrated treaty of alliance, negotiated mainly through his instrumentality, is well known to every one conversant with our early national career. His connection with the convention that framed the Constitution is also valuable subject matter of history. He was eighty-one years of age when a delegate to the latter position, the oldest member of that body. In 1788 he withdrew from public life, his great age rendering retirement desirable. He had two children, a son and a daughter. The son under the British government was appointed Governor of New Jersey, and at the commencement of the Revolution took up his residence in England, where he spent the remainder of his life. The daughter was married to an accomplished gentleman of Philadelphia, Mr. William Bache.

Dr. Franklin died in Philadelphia on the 17th of April, 1790, aged 84 years. His death produced the most profound sensation throughout the country, and it was computed that not less than twenty thousand persons attended the funeral. He was ad-

mired and revered next to Washington. Congress
directed a general mourning for him throughout
the United States for the space of a month, and the
National Assembly of France testified their sense of
the loss which the whole world had sustained by
decreeing that each member should wear mourning
for three days. Genuine grief for the loss of the
great and good man was universal.

In reviewing the imperfect synopsis we have
given of the leading points in the life of this great
man who contributed so much to Colonial, State,
and National history, indeed for the universal brotherhood of man, one cannot fail to admire his many
sterling, genuine traits of character. His *individuality*, that characteristic of all great minds, is most
marked. His resolute will bade defiance to every
obstacle in his path, bounding swallow-like through
sunshine and cloud with almost mathematical celerity and certainty. *Such minds never fail.* His most
wonderful *executive* powers also stand out in bold
relief. His labor triumphs and achievements are
astounding and almost incomprehensible to the ordinary mind. View his whole life from any stand-
point we may desire, as mechanic, inventor, public
official, diplomat, statesman or philanthropist, and
the golden fruits of his versatile life are rich, mellow,
and abundant. His whole life was one of continuous hard work. He abhorred fashionable laziness
and sickly sentimentalism, never calling on Hercules,
but relying on his own strong shoulder to make the

wheels move. Then, again, his sobriety assisted him in his physical and mental labors, for Franklin, although not noisy and demonstrative, was a practical, conscientious temperance man. He considered intemperance the great enemy of the laboring classes, demoralizing and robbing them of their hard earnings; and he advocated this, as he did all practical reforms, without fear or favor. His *integrity*, however, was the brightest jewel in the casket, for in all his private and public relations Franklin was scrupulously an honest man, abhorring debt, always fortifying his honor behind the entrenchments of prudence and economy. His loyalty was above suspicion, and his efforts to assist his sorrow-stricken country in her hours of darkness and distress should be familiar to every American school-boy. At no period of his life was he wealthy, but always in what might be termed comfortable circumstances. Mere crude wealth, divorced from nobler aspirations, is always flimsy and ephemeral, but well-directed intellect has the world as its auditory and lives forever in history. The titled Colonial aristocracy of our early career, and the dazzling millionaires of our more advanced history, are nameless and forgotten, but their humble contemporary—the penniless Franklin—will be remembered as long as science has a friend and honest loyalty an admirer. It is perhaps a lamentable but nevertheless an historical fact which cannot be ignored, that on the occasion of the passage of the

Declaration of Independence there was considerable absenteeism, and a tremendous outside pressure to prevent its consummation. We will return to this part of our subject matter in a future article, and simply refer to it now to state that, although others, and many of them, were absent through real or fictitious cause, Benjamin Franklin, of Pennsylvania, was always at his post of duty, calm and serene, but firm and immovable as the cliffs of Gibraltar.

EVENTS IN THE LIFE OF JOHN MORTON.

The Man who held the balance of power in the Pennsylvania Delegation at the time of the passage of the Declaration of Independence, as described almost a century after his death—His services in the General Assembly and Congress—Some well-authenticated facts connected with the history of our Colonial severance.

IN the quiet cemetery of St. James' Church, in the thrifty young city of Chester, on the Delaware, repose the remains of John Morton, one of the Pennsylvania signers of the Declaration of Independence. It is subject-matter of history, and true beyond cavil, that this same John Morton, at the time of our Colonial severance, by his ballot, held the balance of power in the Pennsylvania delegation, and by his single vote, if he had so desired, could have defeated the *unanimous* passage of the Declaration of Independence. By his intrepidity the social compact was sealed as a *unit*, and our career as a Republic inaugurated. The defection of a single State at this thrilling crisis would have endangered the success of the whole grand movement, and thus completely changed the current of our national history.

A plain, practical, good man, of great personal purity, strict integrity, and marked decision of character, John Morton played no unimportant part in the early history of his country. With an instinctive love of freedom, he combined intense moral sensibility, and a conscientiousness which never allowed him, under the most trying circumstances, to swerve a hair's breadth from what he conceived to be the path of duty. These are the kindred elements and characteristics which in the past have given to religion and patriotism their martyrs and heroes. Before entering somewhat into detail as regards the many interesting events connected with the life of Judge Morton, some well-authenticated facts connected with the history of the Declaration may not prove uninteresting to the general reader. The prevailing popular opinion is that immediately on the passage of the historic document, July 4, 1776, it was signed on that day by the members whose names are affixed. Such, however, is not the fact; not a single name was attached to it at that time. Fifteen days thereafter Congress ordered that it be engrossed on parchment and signed by every member. This was done on the 2d of the following August, almost thirty days after its original passage. It was on that day signed by all who were then members, and afterwards by several who were subsequently elected. A number who voted for the Declaration did not sign it on August 2d for in the interim their respective terms of office had expired.

Strange to say, among those who subscribed their names was one who opposed its passage—Hon. Geo. Reed, of Delaware.

The Pennsylvania delegation on this memorable occasion consisted of seven members, Messrs. Benjamin Franklin, James Wilson, John Morton, John Dickinson, Robert Morris, Thos. Willing, and Chas. Humphreys. All arguments on the matter being exhausted, Congress resolved itself into a Committee of the Whole July 1, 1776. Without any preliminary skirmishing, the chairman, to test the matter, put the question direct to the convention, and all the States voted in the affirmative except Pennsylvania and Delaware, which gave the negative vote. Of the seven Pennsylvanians present, Morton, Franklin, and Wilson voted in favor of, and Dickinson, Morris, Willing, and Humphreys in opposition to the measure. Delaware was a tie—Thomas McKean (born in Chester county, and afterwards Chief Justice of our Commonwealth) voted in favor of the bill, and George Reed against it, Cæsar Rodney, the third member, being unavoidably absent from his post of duty. On the next Thursday, July 4, 1776, amid the most intense excitement, the vital civil question of the age came before Congress. The scene in the old Independence Hall was morally grand beyond description, and the pulsation of patriotic hearts could almost be heard in the profound stillness imparted by the solemnity of the historic occasion. Even were the Colonial heroes successful in the vote which in a moment was to be taken, their future was fearfully problematic and dark, and *each man knew it well.* They represented a constituency of but three millions of people, scattered over a widely extended domain, with no recognized political *status,* a depleted treasury, a disjointed brotherhood, bankrupt in everything but honest manhood, and bound together by no other bond than common sufferings, common danger, and common necessities. Here was a crisis, for glory or shame, history or the halter. Eleven Colonies voted successively in favor of the measure, and as each Colonial vote was announced, legislative dignity was for a moment dethroned by the suppressed, but still audible exultation of the triumphant patriots. And now, once more, there is almost the stillness of the sepulchre as the Colony of Delaware is called, and, like the lightning flash, all eyes are concentrated on her delegation. There is manifest surprise, and low whisperings and mutterings as the discovery is made that again one of her delegates is absent. The stern voice of the courteous but impartial Speaker commands the clerk to proceed with the vote. McKean, true as steel, voted an emphatic aye, while Reed, his colleague, equally loyal perhaps, but timidly created, rendered a vote for the opposition. At this moment the clatter of horses' feet is heard in front of State House Row, and quickly dismounting from his foaming steed, booted and spurred, the third delegate from little

Delaware, the gallant Cæsar Rodney, rushes into the assembly just in time to make the historic Declaration, thus far, a unit and a success. Anticipating the issue, McKean had dispatched a messenger for Rodney, and the latter, with whip and spur, had ridden eighty miles, from the county of Kent, through marsh and swamp, with the dash and enthusiasm of a Richard Cœur de Leon, until he reached his loyal goal. To this point the friends of the measure had been favored with blue skies and fair weather, but sturdy old Pennsylvania was yet to cast her ponderous vote, and the nervous anxiety as to the result was almost painful. Of the seven members enumerated above as composing her delegation, but five are actually in their seats in the convention. Dickinson and Morris, though present in the hall, are not in their official positions during the calling of the roll. One of the five is even absent temporarily, and John Hancock, surveying the field, resorted to a little excusable legislative strategy, and, in order to kill time until the arrival of the mysterious absentee of the Pennsylvania delegation, was addressing the house on some minor parliamentary point, when the hall-door opened, and the missing delegate entered and quietly took his seat. *That man was John Morton, of Delaware county.* His blanched cheek, quivering lip, and clenched hand indicate a fearful internal struggle. Once more the sound of the Speaker's gavel is heard, silence ordered, and Pennsylvania, the last of the Thirteen

Colonies, and the first in commercial importance, is called upon to record her vote. Franklin votes aye, Willing nay, Wilson aye, and Humphrey nay. When the name of John Morton is called he is for an instant the focus of all eyes. The lip has ceased to quiver, the clenched hand has relaxed, and the blanched cheek is now crimsoned with the hot flush of conscientious resolve, and the utterance of his honest "Aye!" reverberating through the old hall gives him historic fame and confirms the *unanimity* of the Declaration of Independence.

All historical authority, contemporaneous or otherwise, unites in awarding the honor of giving the casting vote to Judge Morton, and it has never been denied by any reputable historiographer. In referring once more to the signers of the Declaration we find that of the *seven* members present from Pennsylvania—present at its passage—but *four* of their names are affixed to it, viz.: Robert Morris, Benjamin Franklin, John Morton, and James Wilson. The other five names subsequently added are Benjamin Rush, George Clymer, James Smith, George Taylor, and George Ross, who were appointed delegates to the Continental Congress by the Legislature, on the 26th of July, 1776.

John Morton deserves to be remembered with peculiar respect by State and Nation. The responsibility he assumed was great, even fearful, should the measure be attended with disastrous consequences, as was then most probable. Every element of a

potential lobby was brought into play to subvert
and 'control his judgment in relation to this vote.
But threats and bribes fell harmless at the feet of
this Christian patriot. Friends, relatives, and neighbors ostracised him socially and politically for what
they were pleased to term his criminal imprudence.
During his last illness, on the very verge of the
eternal world, he requested those who stood around
his bedside to tell his enemies " that the hour would
yet come when it would be acknowledged that his
vote in favor of American independence was the
most illustrious act of his life." Morton was a remarkably sensitive man, but lacked neither individuality nor decision, as the crowning act of his
life testifies. For some time immediately after the
promulgation of the Declaration our army in the
field met with an almost unbroken series of disas-
ters ; and solicitude on this point, coupled with the
local persecutions he suffered, no doubt hastened
his death.

He lived only long enough to witness with a sad
heart the calamities and misfortunes that befel the
national arms in almost all the engagements of 1776
and the spring of 1777, and was not permitted, in
the wisdom of a Higher Power, to witness the
bright sunlight of a glorious peace, enunciated on
the nineteenth of April, 1783, after eight long years
of sanguinary, desolating war. In relation to the
status of a majority of that portion of the members
of the Continental Congress who voted against the

Declaration, it may be remarked that their patriotism was never doubted by their colleagues, their constituents, or reliable history. There were thousands in the country of reliable, worthy, patriotic men, who deemed the agitation of so important a question at that particular time as premature and consequently inexpedient. This was the strong argument adduced by the opponents of the measure in the Continental Congress, timid croakers, but yet at heart genuine patriots, men who ardently desired but yet lacked the moral courage to assert their rights. Such a class is even yet always largely represented in all large deliberative bodies; followers, not leaders; good elements for reinforcements, but poor material for the advance guard. John Morton did not belong to the class to which we have alluded, but was blunt, frank and decided, and voted for independence simply because his conscientious convictions led him in that direction. The opponents of the measure in the Pennsylvania delegation claimed, with some show of reason, that their instructions from the Legislature were of a pacific character and restricted the latitude of personal judgment. It will be remembered that the members of the Continental Congress were elected by the several Colonial Legislatures, and not directly by the people. The following is the closing paragraph of certain instructions issued by the Pennsylvania Legislature to the Congressional delegation on the 9th of November, 1775:

"Though the oppressive measures of the British Parliament and administration have compelled us to resist their violence by force of arms, yet we strictly enjoin you that you, in behalf of this Colony, dissent from and utterly reject any propositions, should such be made, that may cause or lead to a separation from our mother country, or to a change of the form of this Government."

On the 14th of the following June we find additional instructions issued, of which the following is the closing portion: "The happiness of these Colonies has, during the whole course of this fatal controversy, been our first wish—their reconciliation with Great Britain our next. Ardently have we prayed for the accomplishment of both. But if we renounce the one or the other, we humbly trust to the mercies of the Supreme Governor of the Universe, that we shall not stand condemned before His throne, if our choice is determined by that overruling law of self-preservation which His divine wisdom has thought fit to implant in the hearts of His creatures."

The last series of instructions in the main are pointed and decided, couched in language indicating earnest, solemn, religious conviction, and both are signed "by order of the House," John Morton, Speaker. He seems to have interpreted the instructions in his own patriotic and original way.

John Morton was born in 1724, in Ridley township, now Delaware county, formerly a part of Chester county, Pa. The house in which he was born is still standing on the Chester turnpike, (the old Queen's highway,) twelve miles from Philadelphia and three from the city of Chester. His ancestors were of Swedish extraction, and were among the first Swedish emigrants who settled on the banks of the Delaware, below Philadelphia. His father, for whom he was named, died a few months before his birth. His mother some time after was married to an intelligent Englishman, John Sketchley, who possessed more than an ordinary education, and who, with great kindness and consideration, superintended the home education of his bright, promising step-son. His active mind rapidly expanded, and gave great promise of future usefulness. Under the guidance and management of Mr. Sketchley, young Morton became quite a profound mathematician, and very proficient as a surveyor, a profession most admirably adapted to the development of method, system and precision, in both thought and action. He never ceased to remember the kindness of Mr. Sketchley, who was indeed a skillful tutor, and a most faithful guardian and friend.

In 1764 he was commissioned as a justice of the peace, and the same year was sent as a delegate to the General Assembly of Pennsylvania, of which he was, for many years, an influential member, and for some time was Speaker of the Lower House. In 1765 he was appointed by our Legislature to attend the General Congress, assembled in New York, to concert measures for the repeal of the odious stamp act. In 1766 he was appointed sheriff of Chester county, which position he held for three years. In 1772 he was elevated to a seat on the bench of the Supreme Court of Pennsylvania, which honorable position he filled with great dignity and ability. In July, 1774, he was elected a member of the historic Congress that convened in Philadelphia the following September to make one final effort to effect a reconciliation between the Colonies and the mother country. This body was composed of men of profound learning, inflexible firmness, and unblemished private and public character; men who could not be seduced from the straight path of duty by any of the glittering temptations of money or power unfortunately so potential in more modern times. Judge Morton earnestly concurred in all the advanced movements and deliberations of that body, which virtually kindled the fires of the Revolution.

In May, 1775, he took his seat in Congress, and was re-elected in November. In July, 1776, he brilliantly closed his Congressional career by his historic vote in the creation of a *unanimous* Declaration of Independence, to which we have already feebly alluded. In April, 1777, he was attacked by an inflammatory fever, which terminated his life after a few days' illness, at the early age of fifty-four, just nine months after he had given his famous vote in the Continental Congress. John Morton was no ordinary man. To the cool caution of his calm

3

temperament was strongly allied the inflexible will of a Cromwell. A stranger to *cunning*, that ready weapon of small minds, he never viewed any National or State question from the stand-point of selfish policy. Such was his devotion to integrity that he would sacrifice his best personal friend, if that friend blocked his own path of duty. In private life and the social circle he was esteemed and beloved for his intelligent vivacity, unspotted personal character, and sweet Christian virtues. His descendants are widely scattered over the different sections of our country, some lingering around and about the old homestead in Delaware county, whilst others are prominently identified with the leading business interests of Philadelphia.

GEORGE CLYMER'S MARKED TRAITS.

A man who never bought or sought office, who never traduced another's character, and whose devotion to his country developed itself in a long and honorable life—An orphan at seven years—From the counting-room to the head of a leading firm—His record in Congress.

THE same strata of sterling qualities and attractive excellencies appear to have pervaded the characters of the leading men of Pennsylvania, signers and others, who figured in our Revolutionary history. Practical common sense, dignified gravity, intense conscientiousness, and burning patriotic zeal, seem to have permeated every fibre and muscle of those primitive patriots.

Prominent among his compeers for stateliness of manners, elegant courtesy, and that ease and grace which some men seem to inherit, and which others can never acquire, was George Clymer. He was born in Philadelphia, in 1739. His father emigrated to this country from Bristol, England, and married a cultivated lady of Philadelphia. At the early age of seven young Clymer was left an orphan, and Mr. William Coleman, a maternal uncle, a gentleman of refinement and culture, and a prominent merchant,

claimed him as his ward, and personally superintended his early education. The guardian was eminently qualified for his responsible position, and the
young orphan was peculiarly fortunate in securing
in him a proficient tutor and most judicious counsellor and friend. On the completion of his preliminary education he was forthwith inducted into
the counting-room of his worthy uncle, which he
entered, however, under the silent protest of his
own judgment. His genius was poorly adapted to
mercantile life and the dull routine of commercial
pursuits, being more friendly disposed to literary
and scientific aspirations. However, he had too
much good sense and gratitude to openly revolt
against the judgment of his worthy relative, and a
merchant he became. He inaugurated his commercial career by transacting business in the name of
George Clymer, merchant, then in the name of Clymer & Ritchie: then formed a business alliance part-
nership with a Mr. Meredith, and subsequently at the
age of twenty-seven, a matrimonial alliance with the
daughter of his last partner, a lady recognized
among the elite of that period as one of the brilliant
stars in fashionable circles. Mr. Clymer continued
for several years a leading business man in Philadelphia, and, although the bulk of his time was absorbed by the cares and duties of his legitimate
vocation, found sufficient leisure to store his mind
with the general principles of international law,
history, politics and light literature, and a vast

amount of valuable general information. By nature he was a lover of free institutions and a democratic form of government, having implicit faith in the will of the people. At a very early age his feelings were strongly enlisted against the many arbitrary acts of the British government, and when concilia- tory measures failed to secure our rights, and the logic of protest, petition and appeal had become thoroughly exhausted, he was among the first men in Philadelphia to suggest and adopt proper meas- ures of national defence. George Clymer was not a theoretic patriot, feasting amid dreamy visions on hopes that could never be realized, but, like the ma- jority of his colleagues of that period, a practical, aggressive one, and in 1773 accepted a captain's commission of a volunteer company raised for the defence of the province. During that year a cargo of tea was sent out by Great Britain, consigned to certain parties in Philadelphia, for the purpose of indirectly levying a contribution on her citizens without their consent. Its arrival at our wharves created the most intense excitement. A mass or town meeting was called at once, and a committee was appointed, of which George Clymer was chair- man, to wait on the consignees and request them under no circumstances to offer that tea for sale in Philadelphia. The delicate task was faithfully per- formed by the committee, and not an ounce of the tea was allowed to be sold within the limits of the city.

Two years after this (1775) Clymer was appointed a member of the historic Committee on Safety; on the 20th day of July, 1776, he was appointed by the Colonial Legislature a member of the Continental Congress, sixteen days after the passage of the Declaration of Independence. As we have stated, however, in a previous article, he had the honor of affixing his name to that document on the second day of the following month.

His practical business habits received honorable recognition by the Government in September, 1775, when he was appointed at that time, jointly with Mr. Stockton, to inspect and report upon the general condition of the northern wing of our army. In December of the same year the good citizens of Philadelphia were startled by the rumor that the British army was moving rapidly upon them. All was alarm and excitement. Congress, then in session there, deeming discretion the better part of valor, wisely concluded to adjourn at once to Baltimore, and there was no *tie* vote on that question. Robert Morris, George Clymer and George Walton were appointed by Congress a committee to remain in Philadelphia and adopt such measures and transact such business as the extraordinary circumstances of the critical occasion might require. In 1777 he was once more returned to Congress, and so arduous were his duties, and so unremitting his exertions during that session, that his health was seriously impaired, and he was compelled for a brief season

to withdraw from public life. His family resided
at this time in Chester county, some twenty miles
from Philadelphia. During the fall of that year a
roving band of British stragglers attacked his house,
destroying all his furniture, his family with the
greatest difficulty escaping with their lives. Mr.
Clymer himself was in Philadelphia at the time, and
when the invaders reached that city in a few days
they sought out his residence, and with a vulgar, mobocratic spirit, at variance with all recognized rules
of honorable warfare, proceeded to level it to the
ground, and were only dissuaded from their purpose
when informed that the building was a leased one,
in which Mr. Clymer had no financial interest whatever. The fact that he was a shining mark for the
wrath of the ruthless foe is the highest compliment
that could be paid to his unswerving loyalty. But
his country had still more work for the young, untiring patriot, and, in December of the same year,
he was appointed a commissioner, in conjunction
with several other gentlemen, to visit the wilds of
Western Pennsylvania on important business of a
secret and confidential nature. It is generally un-
derstood that the object of this mission was to pre-
serve friendly relations with the Indians of the
border, and enlist some of the more friendly of the
Shawnees and Delawares into the service of the
United States. In 1780 our general army was suf-
fering intensely from a combination of unpropitious
causes, which threatened almost to eventuate in its

disbandment. The suggestive mind of Robert Morris, the financial genius of our early history, originated the old Bank of North America in the city of Philadelphia. This institution subserved many great and good purposes in its early days; revived public credit; promoted internal improvements; but, better than all this, was instrumental, to a very great degree, in relieving the wants of our noble army, whose sufferings at that crisis were almost beyond human endurance. As an expression of its faith in and gratitude to this well-managed financial institution Congress passed a formal resolution in its favor, and pledged the faith of the United States to indemnify all subscriptions to its stock. George Clymer was one of the active minds of this financial experiment that ultimately developed into such grand proportions, and served for many years as one of its most efficient directors. In 1780 we find Mr. Clymer again re-elected or re-appointed to Congress. These renewals of public confidence in him were entirely unsolicited on his part, for in those halcyon days of primitive simplicity the office actually *did* seek the man and not the man the office. For two successive years he served his constituency and State most faithfully, seldom being absent from his post of duty, never allowing personal considerations to interfere with the discharge of his official duties, and never drawing any more compensation than he was honestly entitled to. In 1782 he removed with his family to the old town of Princeton, N. J., for the purpose of educating his family at Nassau Hall, then as now one of the leading collegiate institutions of the land. At the beginning of the war, the old college doors were closed, and faculty and students were scattered, many of them fighting the battles of their country. The venerable Dr. Witherspoon, the patriot-president of the college, had exchanged the pulpit for the forum, and was now a Federal lawmaker in the Continental Congress at Philadelphia. In 1782 it was re-opened, however, and in the quiet village of Princeton, with its literary atmosphere and captivating social attractions, George Clymer settled down to enjoy the peace and luxury of private life after the toils, troubles and privations of a long, busy and eventful public career. In two brief years, however, he responded to another call from his native State, this time to be a representative in her Legislature. Of this body he was an influential member, and was appointed by it to represent the State in the great convention which met to frame the Constitution, which was but lately changed. After its adoption he represented the State once more in a Congressional term of two years, when, declining a renomination, he closed his long, most honorable and highly useful legislative career.

In 1791 Mr. Clymer was placed at the head of the excise department in Pennsylvania, at the time when Congress, judiciously or otherwise, passed a bill imposing a duty on all spirits distilled in the country. This legislation was very unpopular in certain sec-

3*

tions of the country, and was particularly obnoxious
to the citizens of Western Pennsylvania. This dissatisfaction eventuated in what is known as the
"whisky insurrection," and for a time assumed a
most threatening attitude. Mr. Clymer had no taste
for factious broils based on whisky, and soon resigned an office which was very distasteful to him.
In 1796 he was appointed, in connection with Colonels Hawkins and Pickens, to negotiate a treaty
with the Cherokee and Creek Indians in Georgia.
He sailed from Philadelphia, for Savannah, in April
of that year, and narrowly escaped shipwreck by a
violent storm, which continued for several days. He
satisfactorily completed the object of his mission
and returned to Philadelphia, and shortly after retired to that private life he so earnestly coveted.
He subsequently officiated as president of the Philadelphia Bank, the Philadelphia Agricultural Society,
and the Academy of Fine Arts. He died January
23, 1818, in the 74th year of his age. George Clymer was a little above the medium size, of fair com-
plexion, and erect and manly in his personal bearing. His marked features indicated intelligence and
benevolence, and resolution without arrogance. He
possessed all that delicacy and sensibility so essential
to taste, and was always an active friend of the fine
arts and polite literature. He was a man of warm
feelings, ardent in his affections, and the very life of
the social circle. Modest and diffident, he was no orator, but a writer of considerable force and elegance.

There was a simplicity and frank honesty in his whole character well calculated to win the friendship of all with whom he came in contact. This charming trait, so rare in public men, was never blunted or blurred by contact with the rude elements of the rough outside world. He never bought or sought office, and scorned to practice the duplicity of the demagogue as the condition of any political preferment he ever received. He never spoke ill of the absent, never traduced any man's character, and in all matters, great or small, was most punctilious and exact in fulfilling all his promises. Socially connected with some of the leading families of Philadelphia in her early history, the home of Mr. Clymer was the abode of taste, wealth, and generous hospitality. In all the varied spheres of life, in the public arena of politics or the quiet elegance of his own home, he was a man whose purity of character was unquestionable, and whose devotion to his country developed itself in a long, honorable life, devoted to her best interests.

JAMES SMITH, IRISH AMERICAN.

A man practical and prudent in his loyal career, and brimful of that mother wit for which his race is proverbial—From College to the law office—An uncompromising advocate of prompt and vigorous measures—Colonel in the Army, member of the Provincial Convention of 1775, and one of the body to frame the first Constitution of Pennsylvania.

AN interesting and somewhat remarkable fact, connected not only with the Pennsylvania signers of the Declaration, but with all of them, was their astonishing longevity. They numbered fifty six persons and averaged sixty five years. Four of the number attained the age of ninety and upwards, fourteen exceeded eighty years, and twenty-three reached the venerable Psalmist's standard of three-score and ten. The fourteen members composing the New England delegation averaged seventy-five years. Charles Carroll, of Carrollton, was the last survivor of the noble fifty-six. Of the nine signers of the Pennsylvania delegation five were natives of the province, one was born in Delaware, one in Scotland, and two in Ireland. The subject of our memoir, James Smith, was a native of the Emerald Isle, and, although his name has not figured conspicuously in

our Revolutionary history in proportion to his intrinsic merits, was a most worthy gentleman, eminently aggressive, and withal practical and prudent
in his loyal career, and brimful of that mother wit,
the *sauce piquante*, for which the Irish character is
proverbial. One peculiarity of the man was his ret-
icence concerning his age, his most intimate friends
never being able to find out precisely what it was.
Like some stately, fashionable maiden drifting from
the whirlpool of social folly into the misty woodland
of the "sere and yellow leaf," he was conscientiously
opposed to telling any one his age, and pertinaciously
and often bluntly refused to impart the secret to a
living soul—a secret which was buried with him in
his grave. His friends conjectured that he was born
between the years 1715 and 1720.

All that vast territory in Pennsylvania lying west
of the Susquehanna, now abounding in blooming
valleys, rich in agricultural wealth, dotted with
smiling villages and thrifty cities, the church and
academic spires indicating the positive worth and
progressive spirit of the inhabitants, was a century
ago a comparative wilderness. The father of James
Smith, tired of the shackles and bondage of foreign
despotism, left the shores of his native isle, and with
a numerous family located in this unattractive waste,
exiled as it were from all the comforts and luxuries
of social life. They settled in 1743 in the old
historic county of Cumberland, now one of the most
beautiful of Southern Pennsylvania, where for many

years they buffeted the storms and adversities of rough frontier life. Placing that high estimate on liberal education which appears to have been a strong characteristic of our primitive forefathers, he selected from his family group his son James and placed him under the educational control of the distinguished Dr. Allison, then provost of the College of Philadelphia, who appears to have been the universal Colonial schoolmaster of the period. The classical proficiency of young Smith was of a high order, but he gave special attention to surveying, then one of the useful and practical professions of the day, and for which there was an unlimited demand.

After completing his collegiate course in Philadelphia he removed to Lancaster, then one of the outposts of civilization, and entered the office of Thomas Cookson, Esq., as a law student. On his admission to the bar he removed to the old village of Shippensburgh, at that time the court town of Cumberland county, and a point of considerable business importance. Remaining here for a short time his restless ambition yearned for a wider field of operation, and he removed to the thrifty town of York, Pa., where he permanently established himself, and where he successfully practiced his profession during the balance of his life. At the very inauguration of the contest between Great Britain and the Colonies, the latter found a firm friend and gallant champion in the brilliant young lawyer of York, a representative man of the rough, strong, honest elements of the rural districts of the wild frontier. In 1774, at the delegate meeting of all the counties of the State, convened to give an expression of public sentiment on the propriety and expediency of abstaining from the importation of any goods from England, James Smith was the representative from York, and was one of a committee appointed to draft instructions to the General Assembly, then about to convene.

There is no disguising the fact that a most powerful effort was being made by the friends of unconditional peace to suppress anything like a public outbreak between the two countries. Many of these parties were actuated by the purest motives imaginable, and these were encouraged by others naturally cautious and timid, representatives of that large ratio of society lacking moral courage whenever it is essentially desirable, nervously receiving every incident as an accident, and every accident as a positive calamity. The impulsive loyalty of Smith, perhaps, drove him to the other extreme, and made him an uncompromising advocate of prompt and vigorous measures. After the adjournment of the convention to which allusion has been made, he returned in 1774 to York, and organized the first volunteer militia company ever raised in Pennsylvania in opposition to the forces of Great Britain. He was elected captain of this company, and subsequently colonel of a regiment to which it became attached. Colonel Smith was a member of the

Provincial Convention of January, 1775, and one
of the ablest champions of the spirited declaration
made by that body, viz.: that "if the British administration should determine by force to effect a
submission to the late arbitrary acts of the British
Parliament, in such a situation we hold it as an indispensable duty to resist such force, and at every
hazard to defend the rights and liberties of America." This resolution had the true ring of defiant
resistance to despotic usurpation; but, strange as it
may seem, it was practically ignored by a series of
instructions issued November 9, of the same year,
by the General Assembly to the delegates appointed
by it to Congress. The tenor of these instructions
was not hidden, as the following positive resolution
indicates: "That though the oppressive measures of
the British Parliament and administration have
compelled us to resist their violence by force of
arms, yet we strictly enjoin you that you, in behalf
of this colony, dissent from and utterly reject any
proposition, should such be made, that may cause or
lead to a separation from our mother country or a
change in the form of government." The dominant
Quaker element, actuated, no doubt, by conscientious motives, was mainly instrumental in securing
the passage of this strangely constructed resolution.
Here was a dead-lock, a broad antagonism, one cloud
charged with positive, the other with negative electricity, in close proximity, with a collision inevita-
ble. The shock and reverberation came on the 15th

of May, 1776, when Congress adopted a resolution
which almost amounted to a separation. The citizens of Philadelphia assembled *en masse* five days
after the passage of the resolution, and in front of
the very building in which Congress was assembled,
discussed and digested plans of positive resistance.
The wildest enthusiasm prevailed, and Chestnut
street was crowded with the excited populace, clam-
oring for an immediate dissolution of our Colonial
relations and "war to the hilt." The instructions
of the Provincial Assembly were not only pointedly
condemned, but hooted and spurned by the excited
multitude, and a loud demand made for a Provincial
Conference to establish a new form of government
in Pennsylvania. This conference met on the 18th
of June, 1776, and was composed of the advance
guard, the progressive, intelligent young men of the
State. Among these was James Smith, of York,
manfully struggling in the front ranks for a clear
definition of our national rights, and how to promptly secure them. On the fourteenth of the same
month, four days before the meeting of this conference, the General Assembly had rescinded their ill-
timed and obnoxious instructions to the delegates
in Congress by an able and dignified State paper in
the form of a resolution, closing thus: "The happiness of these Colonies has, during the whole course
of this fatal controversy, been our first wish, their
reconciliation with Great Britain our next. Ardently have we prayed for the accomplishment of

both. But, if we renounce the one or the other, we humbly trust to the mercies of the Supreme Governor of the Universe, that we shall not stand condemned before His throne if our choice is determined by that law of self-preservation which His Divine wisdom has thought fit to implant in the hearts of His creatures." This was signed "by order of the House, John Morton, Speaker." This prompt action of the Assembly would seem to have obviated the necessity of the special conference meeting, but meet they did, determined to give formal expression of their views in relation to the anticipated Declaration of Independence. To accomplish this a motion was made by Dr. Benjamin Rush, then comparatively a young man, which was seconded by Col. James Smith; and these two gentlemen, in connection with the impulsive but brilliant Thomas McKean, were appointed a committee to draft a clear, explicit declaration of their views on the matter. On the following morning they made their report, which, being unanimously confirmed by the conference and signed by the members, was transmitted to Congress on June the 25th, a day or two before the Declaration of Independence by Congress was presented to that body. This document, with which Col. Smith was very closely identified, bears a marked resemblance to the original as drafted by Jefferson and promulgated by Congress, July 4, 1776.

In the early part of July a Convention assembled

in Philadelphia to frame a Constitution for the State, and on the 15th instant Colonel Smith appeared and took his seat as a member of that body. Five days thereafter he was elected by the convention a member of Congress, which position he held for several years, and in which he was considered strong, efficient, and incorruptible. After his withdrawal from Congress he resumed his professional pursuits, until 1800, when he retired from the bar, after a successful career of sixty years, untarnished by a single dishonorable or disreputable episode.

Colonel Smith was an eccentric person, of peculiar traits, remarkable for his love of sport and well-regulated conviviality. His satire was keen as a Damascus blade, and his humor inimitable, and in either sphere he was unsurpassed by Lucian, Swift, or Rabelais. He was a sanguine, hopeful, cheerful man, always searching for sunlight instead of clouds, his genial presence imparting almost fragrance, stimulating the despondent, and strengthening the doubtful amidst the many adversities and revolutions of the stirring times in which he lived. His memory was uncommonly retentive, and his mind well stored with humorous incidents and anecdotes, which he recited, when prudence and judgment dictated, with marked effect. His acquirements, however, were not by any means of a superficial character, for he was learned in the law, and a man of broad, comprehensive, statesmanlike views, a valuable acquisition to the many honorable bodies

with which he was officially connected.   His loyalty
was unfaltering and uncompromising, and he cheerfully signed his name to the charter of our liberties,
without doubt, cavil, or criticism.   He died in 1806,
at the supposed age of eighty-six.

GEORGE TAYLOR OF PENNSYLVANIA.

From the atmosphere of tinctures and lotions to an iron foundry as an ordinary day laborer—Next, proprietor of a whole establishment—The result of prudence, tact, economy, and industry—A Representative of Northampton county in the Provincial Assembly—Taylor's Congressional career, &c.

THE life of George Taylor furnishes an illustrious example of the natural powers of a strong, rugged mind triumphing over the deficiencies of early education, and marching straight forward in the path of honor and distinction, regardless of every intervening obstacle. Notwithstanding the veil of oblivion obscures the minute details of this plain, practical, but honest and useful life, baffling the ingenuity of the biographer, his fame as one of the signers of the Declaration is embalmed in the national heart. Although an eminently useful man in our early history, a fine parliamentarian, peerless as an executive officer in the committee room, thoroughly reliable in all startling crises, his long official career, unstained by a single blot of corruption, there is no man in American history about whom so little is known as George Taylor. No gilt-edged eulogium perpetuates his virtues, but his acts and

deeds can only be found in the dusty records and archives of our Colonial history.   One of the nine distinguished representatives of Pennsylvania who affixed his signature to the charter of our liberties,
he is to-day almost forgotten, save through the medium of some brief, imperfect, unsatisfactory sketch.

> "What is glory?—in the socket
> See how dying tapers flare."

Mr. Taylor was born in the North of Ireland in
1716.   His father was a highly respectable minister,
of more than ordinary culture, with a keen appreciation of the advantages of a good education.   He
gave his son an opportunity to improve his mind,
and after some preliminary preparation the young
man commenced the study of medicine.   He soon,
however, became disgusted with his new profession,
and sooner than be classified as a

> Quack-salving, cheating mountebank, whose skill
> Would make the sound men sick, and sick men kill,

abandoned the atmosphere of tinctures and lotions
for a sphere of more variety and activity.   About
the year 1736, without a penny or an outfit, he went
on board a ship sailing for New York, and was registered as a redemptioner, and on his arrival his
services were sold, under certain stipulations to a
Mr. Savage, the proprietor of extensive iron works
in the old town of Durham, a few miles from Easton, Pa.   Here he was employed for some time as an
ordinary day laborer, his specific work being that

of a "filler" throwing coal into a furnace when in blast.

In this uncongenial and trying position he never uttered a complaint, although the work was rough and his surroundings generally disagreeable. His employer soon transferred him from these menial duties to his own private office, where he was exceedingly useful, and where he remained for several years. On the death of Mr. Savage young Taylor became connected in marriage with his widow, and consequently the proprietor of the whole establishment. In his new sphere, suddenly elevated from comparative poverty to financial independence, he exhibited great prudence, tact, economy and industry, and in a short time amassed a. very large fortune. In a few years he purchased an additional estate on the Lehigh river, in Northampton county, where he erected a spacious mansion, and took up his permanent residence. Here he was first called into public life, and represented Northampton county in the Provincial Assembly, which met in Philadelphia, October, 15, 1764, of which body he was appointed a member of the Committee of Grievances, and where he displayed very considerable legislative capacity. In June, 1765, the Speaker of the Assembly received a proposal from the House of Representatives of Massachusetts Bay, soliciting a general Congress of Delegates to convene in New York city the ensuing fall. At the meeting of the Pennsylvania Assembly, in September, of the same year, this proposition was agreed to, and the Speaker, Mr. Fox, Mr. Dickinson, Mr. Bryan, and John Morton were elected delegates to represent the Colony. An additional committee was appointed to draft instructions for the government of this important delegation. George Taylor was a member of this latter committee, and his prudent suggestions and practical views had great force and consideration in framing these instructions. In 1765 he was re-elected a Representative to the Provincial Assembly from Northampton county, and participated in the leading questions and measures then introduced. In June, 1766, we find him one of a committee to prepare an address of thanks to the King on the repeal of the Stamp Act. From 1764 to 1770 Mr. Taylor was very closely identified with our provincial legislation, serving frequently and honorably on many very important committees, such as "amending the judiciary establishment," "to regulate the assessment of taxes," "to investigate the rights of the House," "to choose the printer of the public laws," "to raise loans on bills of credit" and "to prepare a system to improve the navigation of of our great rivers." In 1766 he made strenuous efforts to bring to the bar of public justice some "regulators" of our Colonial borders who had wilfully and maliciously, without the least shadow of pretext or provocation, murdered in cold blood some Indians. This outrage almost precipitated a collision between the province and the Indians. Mr.

Taylor presented a strong address to the Governor on the subject, who gave it as much consideration as his conservative and dilatory character could consistently allow. In 1775 he was actively employed in developing his iron interests in Northampton, but met with such poor success that in order to recruit his failing fortune he was compelled to return to Durham, the scene of his former prosperity. Here he acted as an associate judge of the county court, and was appointed Colonel of militia. In October, 1775, he took his seat once more as a member of the Provincial Assembly, where he served as a member of the committees on "Crown Grants," "Connecticut Claims," "Procuring Arms," and as an honorable member of the historic Committee of Safety, then and since recognized as the great revolutionary organ of the government. On November 4, 1775, the Assembly elected delegates to the succeeding Continental Congress, and Mr. Taylor, in connection with several other prominent gentlemen, was appointed to draft a set of instructions for them. The circumstances surrounding the Colony of Pennsylvania at that time were of a very singular character. She had not felt so keenly the despotic heel of the oppressor as some of the other Colonies, her constitution was free and liberal, and her proprietary form of government was by no means oppressive. She had on more than one occasion been specially favored by the Crown, and peace and general prosperity prevailed within her borders. These and

4

other considerations created at that particular time a conservative sentiment bordering on a strong reluctance to sever the bond so long uniting her to the mother country. Hence, the series of instructions emanating from this committee of seven, of a conciliatory character, urging its members to seek all honorable means for the redress of American grievances, but not to do anything to widen the breach and destroy that harmony and union which was so essential to the welfare of both countries. However, during the winter and spring of 1776 there was a great reaction in public sentiment throughout the length and breadth of her provincial borders, eventuating in the Assembly rescinding their former instructions, and declaring firmly and boldly that they were unwilling to purchase peace by a dishonorable submission to arbitrary power. These latter instructions, which had the ring of sterling patriotism, authorized the Pennsylvania Representatives "to concur with the other delegates in Congress in forming such further compacts between the united Colonies, concluding such treaties with foreign kingdoms and States, and in adopting such other measures as, upon a view of all circumstances, shall be judged necessary for promoting the liberty, safety and interests of America, reserving to the people of this Colony the sole and exclusive right of regulating the internal government and policy of the same." These instructions were adopted by the Assembly, June 14, 1776, and were a powerful auxiliary in promoting

the passage of the Declaration on the 4th of the
ensuing month. The approbation of Pennsylvania
was only obtained by the casting vote of the Hon.
John Morton. On the 20th of July the Pennsylvania Assembly proceeded to a new choice of Representatives, and those who had opposed the passage of the Declaration were dropped from the rolls,
and in their stead were appointed Messrs. Taylor,
Ross, Clymer, Rush and Smith. The Declaration
was passed and proclaimed July 4, but the copy
engrossed on parchment was not prepared until
nearly a month after. The gentlemen named above,
although not present at its formal passage, had the
honor of affixing their names to it August 2, 1776,
at which time it was signed by the members generally. In his Congressional career George Taylor
was noted for his sagacity, decision, patriotism, and
fine executive powers. In March, 1777, he retired
from Congress and repaired to Easton, where he
concentrated his energies in recuperating his private
fortune, and with very great success. He never entered the political arena or the legislative hall afterwards. It was glory enough for him to see his
once subjugated and impoverished country swiftly
and surely developing into an honorable position
among the nations of the earth; and it was the crowning honor of his whole life to be permitted to sign
his honest name to the Magna Charta of our liberties. He died on the 23d of February, 1781, in the
sixty-sixth year of his age.

JAMES WILSON, OF PENNSYLVANIA.

Student in the schools of Edinburgh and St. Andrew, tutor in the Philadelphia College, member of the Bar, delegate to the Provincial Convention of the State, elected to Congress, and Advocate General for France in America—Accusations sufficiently disproved by history.

TO the multitude the name of James Wilson, of Pennsylvania, is not a familiar one. Many others, far less deserving, have been perpetuated in history under the misnomer of fame. To the well-versed student of general jurisprudence and the intelligent reader of our primitive Colonial and Revolutionary times, his name and fame are familiar, and to such he needs no special introduction. Born in 1742, in Scotland, the home of Wallace and Bruce, of Burns and Sir Walter Scott, the abode of stubborn but consistent theology, cultivated fiction and gentle song, he was fortunate in securing very great educational advantages. His father resided in the neighborhood of St. Andrew's, and although not wealthy, was possessed of that moderate competency which, when coupled with a contented disposition, is oftentimes more productive of real comfort than the inheritance of a kingdom. Within the classic walls of the celebrated schools of Edinburgh and St. Andrew's, young Wilson, taking advantage of fortuitous circumstances, studied with an untiring will and received a superior education. James Wilson was a natural-born republican and a lover of free institutions. At the age of twenty-four he resolved to leave his native land and seek fortune and fame in the wilderness of America. In the spring of 1766 he arrived in the city of Philadelphia, with a full supply of recommendations from prominent men in Scotland to leading men here. He was not long in securing a position, for in less than three months after his arrival he was appointed tutor in the Philadelphia College, where he remained for some time, and was recognized as one of the most efficient classical scholars that had ever been identified with the institution. By assiduous application to his professional duties, the cultivation of a good character, and possessing genial, fascinating personal manners, he attracted the attention of some of the leading men of the metropolis, who were generously awaiting to afford him any facilities required to promote his success. By the joint influence of the learned and good Bishop White and Judge Peters, he was afforded an opportunity of entering the office of the celebrated lawyer, John Dickinson, who received his own professional training at the Temple, in London, and was widely known as a writer of mark and a most profound jurist. Dickinson was the author of the celebrated "Farmer's Letters," written in 1767–

68, and although his political history is somewhat
blurred by his peculiar views in relation to the passage of the Declaration of Independence, he was in
the main a sound, loyal man, possessing a highly
cultivated mind, refined taste, habitual eloquence,
and polished elegance of manners. Young Wilson
was fortunate in securing such a worthy preceptor,
and for two years he applied himself to his legal
studies with great zeal and industry. Immediately
after his admission to the bar he left Philadelphia
and settled in Reading, at that time a very small,
retired village. He remained there, however, but
a short time, and then removed to the venerable
borough of Carlisle, in Cumberland County, where
he practiced with very great success for several
years and acquired the reputation of being a most
eminent counsellor. He removed afterwards to Annapolis, Md., whence he came to Philadelphia in
1778, where he continued permanently to reside
during the remainder of his life. In 1774 he was
a member of the Provincial Convention of Pennsylvania, and, in connection with Mr. Dickinson,
was nominated as a delegate to Congress. Both,
however, were defeated through the manipulation and
intrigue of Speaker Galloway, a gentleman of very
strongly suspected loyalty, who afterwards allied
himself with the British when they occupied Philadelphia. In the following year Mr. Wilson was
elected to Congress, and took his seat in that body
May 10, 1775. Here he remained for two years,

doing good official duty, when he was removed through the intense partisan feeling then prevailing. In thé fall of 1782, however, he was re-elected, and took his seat January 2, 1783. Mr. Wilson was at this particular period in the very zenith of his professional glory, and was considered by all odds the best lawyer in the whole Commonwealth. At that time a serious controversy was going on between Pennsylvania and Connecticut about the proper title to certain valuable lands claimed by the latter State and located within the charter boundary of the former. In this important controversy Mr. Wilson was appointed by the Supreme Executive Council to take charge of the interests of Pennsylvania. A court of commissioners was appointed to determine the rightful claimant, and December 30, 1782, the great question came up before that body at Trenton, N. J. On this occasion Mr. Wilson put forth his ablest efforts, and by a luminous and impressive argument, which occupied the attention of the court for four days, successfully carried his point, and received from the learned commission a unanimous decision in favor of the claims of Pennsylvania. As corroborative of the very high legal character enjoyed by Mr. Wilson, it may be remarked that he received at this period from the French Government the important appointment of advocate general for France in this country. He was thus commissioned June 5, 1779, and for two years performed its requirements with honor and credit, when he resigned on account of some minor disagreement about his official pay. He continued, however, subsequently to transact much consular and other important business for the French government, and the King, as a slight compensation for his valuable services, gave him ten thousand livres. In addition to being an intellectual giant in his chosen profession, Mr. Wilson was a most capable and trustworthy representative of the people in Congress. He steered clear of all subsidies, bounties, and bribes, and studied well the wants and interests of his constituents. His general business habits were of a superior order, and in the committee-room, being sagacious, faithful, and industrious, he worked assiduously and effectually, with the quiet system of a well-regulated machine. Such elements, combined with strong native talent and a mind most admirably trained, produced him much fame, and, as a consequence, no little persecution. In proportion as he rose in public estimation was he calumniated and slandered by puny rivals whom he had quietly but rapidly outrun in the race for professional and political honors.

" Base envy, withers at another's joy,
And hates the excellence it cannot reach."

Two specific charges seem to have been made by this class of humanitarians against James Wilson. He was accused of being secretly opposed to the Declaration of Independence, and also of being one of a hostile combination organized against Washington in 1777. History furnishes sufficient denial through the official records of the Government to the first charge, which was as foundationless as "the baseless fabric of a dream." On the first of July, 1776, as we have stated in a former article, when the grave question was discussed in Committee of the Whole, and received the votes of all but two States, James Wilson's record is clear and unimpeachable; he voted in the affirmative. On the memorable fourth of the same month, when the question was revived once more, Franklin, Morton, and James Wilson voted in favor of the sterling measure, and thus secured a unanimous vote of the thirteen colonies in favor of its passage.

As to the second charge, it was equally unfounded. The conspiracy against General Washington, which most certainly did exist, was more of a military than of a civil character. Washington, by a series of brilliant, rapid strides, reached the very summit of human exaltation, and was justly termed the idol of the nation. The recital of his troubles at this particular period furnishes the same old story with which history abounds. As long as victory perched upon his banner his life was one continuous, magnificent ovation; but when disaster came with its chilling blasts and threatening clouds, the firm friends of yesterday fell thick and fast around him "like leaves in Valumbrosa." When reverses overtook his special command, General Gates with the northern wing was acquiring additional fame by the capitulation of Saratoga; the latter, flushed with

4*

success, coveted the coronet another wore, and dimmed the lustre of all his military achievements by the unsoldierly and unfriendly attitude he assumed towards George Washington. In this unworthy crusade he was assisted by some subordinate officers, and not a few members of Congress. But among them all there is no evidence whatever to implicate James Wilson, and nothing to compromise his reputation as a staunch friend of the great chieftain. Generals Gates and Conway were really the prime movers in the whole disgraceful conspiracy against Washington, but the latter had a strong hold on public favor which he had gallantly and honestly earned, and a fierce reaction soon set in and once more entrenched him firmly in the affections of the whole nation. Gates, whose vaulting ambition had sadly overleapt itself, dwindled into comparative obscurity, which was somewhat accelerated by his disastrous defeat at Camden. Conway, the champion calumniator of the period, scorned by all honorable men for his gross abuse of one who occupied such a worthy and honorable place in the nation, being charged with palpable cowardice at the battle of Germantown, resigned his commission April 28, 1778, and quietly drifted into oblivion.

Wilson was a brilliant member of the Constitutional Convention of 1787, and, being a man of sagacity and foresight, a profound lawyer of great tact, and a fluent, forcible speaker, did as much as any one man in that famed body for the creation of the Constitution under which we now exist. Nay, more, on the 23d of July, 1787, it was resolved "That the proceedings of the convention for the establishment of a National Government, except what respects the Supreme Executive, be referred to a committee for the purpose of reporting a Constitution conformably to the proceedings afore-said." Of this most important committee James Wilson was chairman, and on the 6th of August they reported the Constitution. This was a high honor conferred on Pennsylvania, and its noble ap-pointee fulfilled his commission in a manner worthy the great Commonwealth he represented. Mr. Wil-son was subsequently a member of the State Legis-lature, when the important duty devolved upon it of ratifying the general Constitution, and here again his experience as a legislator and erudition as a law-yer made him eminently useful. After the Federal Constitution was ratified, a convention was called to make our State Constitution harmonize with that of the General Government, and Mr. Wilson was one of a committee appointed to make the necessary change, and upon him rested the task of making the draft. In corroboration of what we have before in-timated as to the good feeling existing between Washington and himself, in 1789 the former ap-pointed him a justice of the Supreme Court of the United States. The bench at that time was pro-verbially strong. John Jay was Chief Justice, and his colleagues were ex-Chief Justice Cushing, of

Massachusetts; ex-Chief Justice Harrison, of Maryland (formerly one of the confidential secretaries of Washington); ex-Judge Blair, of Virginia; John Rutledge, the accomplished scholar and statesman of South Carolina, and James Wilson, of Pennsylvania. This was an array of almost unparalleled intellectual brilliancy, but plain James Wilson, of Pennsylvania, was the peer of any man who sat in that court. He officiated in this high and honorable position for nine years. While attending court as a United States Circuit Judge in 1798, in Edenton, North Carolina, he was taken suddenly ill and died there, aged fifty-six years. Judge Wilson was a man about six feet in stature, of fine personal appearance and graceful demeanor. He was a shining member of the Philadelphia bar in its comparative infancy, and as a citizen and gentleman was noted for his graceful courtesy and genial hospitality. He was always distinguished for great integrity of character and an inviolate regard for truth. He was twice married, and many of his honorable descendants are yet living in the States of New York and Pennsylvania.

HON. GEORGE ROSS, ATTORNEY-AT-LAW.

The result of fifteen years' practice in Lancaster county—Prosecutor to the King and Representative to the Pennsylvania Assembly—Points in his career as a Legislator—An ardent supporter of the demand for a General Congress—Member of the Committee of Grievances and of the General Convention, &c., &c.

THIS gentleman, whose name is the last of the Pennsylvania delegation affixed to the Declaration of Independence, was the son of the Rev. George Ross, rector of the Episcopal church in the old town of New Castle, Delaware. He was born in 1730, and his youth was characterized by an unusual fondness for literature and thirst for learning. His worthy father, a gentleman of culture and education, accorded to the son every advantage his circumstances would permit to develop and improve his literary tastes. Fortified by cherished home principles and the best educational facilities the village could afford, young Ross, at the early age of eighteen, enrolled himself as a law student in the office of his brother, John Ross, Esq., at that time a promising lawyer in the city of Philadelphia. After devoting three years of untiring study to his

new profession he determined to risk his fortune in
the old frontier town of Lancaster, at that time near
the western limits of civilization. He timidly shrunk
from the formidable competition of the Philadelphia
bar, which, even at that early day, strange as it may
seem, was in the very zenith of its professional glory,
including in its membership the most brilliant lawyers of the whole country. George Ross went to ·
the Far West in Lancaster county, armed and
equipped with a good character and a superior education, and linked his youthful fortune with the
humble, honest yeomanry of that distant land, now
accessible in two hours by rail from Philadelphia.
He settled there in 1751, and soon married Miss
Ann Lawler, an accomplished and cultivated young
lady residing in his newly adopted home.

For fifteen long years he devoted his undivided
time and energies to his profession, intellectual capital well invested, producing him in return a large
and lucrative practice, and for a short-term the
honorable local office of prosecutor to the King.
During all this time he eschewed politics, entering
its fascinating arena in 1768, when he was elected a
Representative from Lancaster county to the Pennsylvania Assembly, taking his seat in October of
the same year. He remained in this position for
several consecutive years, and won the respect of
his colleagues of all political shades, and the approbation of an intelligent constituency. Whilst there
he made the Indian question a special study. This

theme was as vexatious a one in old as it has been
in modern times, and was a subject of constant anxiety to the province, producing oftentimes very great
differences between the Assembly and the Govern-
ors.   It was a sort of standing controversial question for the political magnates to fall back upon
when they had a superabundance of leisure time,
which was very often the case.   The Governor frequently interfered in the matter in an arbitrary and
injudicious manner, his motives being good, but his
suggestions being impracticable and decidedly im-
politic.   On one occasion he recommended in his
message an increase of the garrison at Fort Pitt.
The Assembly were marked in their opposition to
this, and their reply, couched in respectful but emphatic language, was prepared by Ross, of Lancaster.   "We all know," it recites, "that from the first
settlement of the province, down to the late French
and Indian war, the most perfect good understanding and friendship were preserved between this
government and those people, by a conduct uniformly just and kind towards them; that since the late
Indian war the like happy effects have been produced by the like policy, and that on the contrary
the maintaining of garrisons in or near their country
has been frequently an object of their jealousy and
complaints.   *   *   *   *   *   *   *   *   *

"We might offer other reasons for not concurring
in sentiment with your Honor on the propriety of
supporting a garrison at Fort Pitt; but, being of

opinion that any warlike preparations, even within our own frontier, at a time of prevailing harmony between us and the natives, may be attended with more ill than good consequences, we shall waive them as unnecessary, and content ourselves with assuring you that we shall, and we have no doubt that all future Assemblies will be very ready, when there shall be real occasion, to afford every kind of protection to the back inhabitants the circumstances of the province will allow."

George Ross, however, was destined by his erudition and force of character to play a more conspicuous part, in a more comprehensive drama, than the maintainance of a petty garrison at Fort Pitt in the Western wilds of Pennsylvania. The arbitrary proceedings of the British government were electrifying the nation, and creating deep, hoarse, colonial mutterings and threats from New Hampshire to the Carolinas. The demand of Virginia and other States for the meeting of a general congress found an ardent supporter in Mr. Ross. The resolutions making this request were received by the Pennsylvania Assembly on the very eve of its dissolution, and on account of their profound importance final action was postponed, and the matter referred to the succeeding Assembly. Mr. Ross was appointed chairman of a committee to communicate this action to the Virginia House of Delegates, which was done in a prompt and courteous manner. In July following a committee of seven on the part of the province was appointed to meet the other colonial delegates at a time and place to be determined. The instructions to this committee by a singular coincidence were drafted by Ross himself, and were positive and concise, giving the honorable appointees considerable discretion and latitude. In obedience to these instructions he took his seat in Congress September 5, 1774, and filled the position until January, 1777, when he obtained leave of absence on account of sickness, and retired. His public career as a Congressional Representative elicited the warmest commendation from his constituents, as is evidenced by the following resolutions passed by the inhabitants of old Lancaster county :

Resolved, That the sum of one hundred and fifty pounds out of the county stock be forthwith transmitted to George Ross, one of the members of Assembly for this county, and one of the delegates for this Colony in the Continental Congress, and that he be requested to accept the same as a testimony from this county of their sense of his attendance on the public business, to his great private loss, and of their approbation of his conduct.

Resolved, That if it be more agreeable, Mr. Ross purchase with part of the said money a genteel piece of plate, one ornamented as he thinks proper, to remain with him as a testimony of the esteem this county has for him, by reason of his patriotic conduct in the great struggle for American liberty.

These resolutions, couched perhaps in plain, homely

phraseology, indicate a patriotic gratitude and great personal confidence on the part of the honest yeomanry of his adopted county, and their presentation was exceedingly gratifying to Mr. Ross. From a positive sense of duty, however, he felt compelled to decline an acceptance of either the pounds or the plate, considering it as he remarked, "the duty of every man, and especially of every representative of the people, to contribute by every means within his power to the welfare of his country, *without expecting pecuniary rewards!*" This was considered sound doctrine in our primitive history, but its symmetry has not only been slightly marred, but very badly damaged, in modern Legislative circles. Although a member of Congress, Mr. Ross was at the same time an active, influential member of the Provincial Legislature. In 1775 the Governor transmitted a message to the House, in which he argued in favor of pacific measures as a good stroke of Colonial policy, in view of the threatening attitude assumed by the mother country. It was a common custom at that time to reply at once to the messages of the Governor, and his present action demanded a public expression of opinion by the different members. The question was whether Pennsylvania would make an humble retraction, or order an uncompromising advance. The talent of the House developed itself in a brilliant debate, and George Ross, as the leading friend of decisive measures, succeeded in securing a committee coinciding with his views, and of which he was a member. This committee presented their report in courteous, but strong terms, and its reception was the signal for an exciting debate, which lasted two days, ending, however, in its adoption by twenty-two to fifteen votes. Strange, that then, as now, numerically strong minorities were always found when great national questions were involved. In the summer of 1775 something more tangible and vigorous was demanded than Legislative resolves—something more formidable than rhetorical display or paper missiles. Keenly appreciative of the crisis, the Assembly appointed Mr. Ross, and several other worthy gentleman, as a committee to "consider and report such measures as they might think proper to place Philadelphia and the Province in a state of defence."

This committee reported promptly, recommending the people to associate for the protection of their lives, liberty, and property.; and strongly urging upon the inhabitants of the province the importance of collecting stores of ammunition and arms. This was the nucleus of the celebrated Committee of Safety, afterwards formed, which did such good practical work in the early days of the Revolution, and of which George Ross was an active and efficient member. This committee was really for a time the potential executive organ of the Government, and was clothed with almost unlimited powers, which it seldom, if ever, abused. He belonged also to the Committee of Grievances, and was appointed, with two others, to prepare rules and regulations for the government of the forces of the province which might be raised.

On the dissolution of the Proprietary government and a substitution of a General Convention for the previous Legislature, Mr. Ross represented Lancaster county in this new body, and was recognized as one of its leading members. In this sphere he was appointed to assist in preparing a declaration of rights for the State, and was chairman of two very important committees—one for framing regulations for the government of the convention; the other for preparing an ordinance declaratory of what should be considered high treason and misprison of treason against the State, and the punishment for the same. In rehearsing briefly the salient points in the career of this distinguished man we notice his great capacity for labor; his untiring industry, as proven by his voluminous work as a committee-man; his sterling integrity, and his genial, unostentatious manners, all indicating a happy blending of the incorruptible statesman and the Colonial patriot. Mr. Ross was well versed in the law, and before the Revolution took high rank in his profession. On its inauguration and during its continuance his sphere was changed from that of mere local subordinate provincial judicature to a higher plane involving the consideration and solution of great and grave national questions. His compeers were gifted, high-toned honorable gentlemen—James Wilson, then of Carlisle, Biddle of Reading, Read, Attorney General Sergent, and Lewis, formed a brilliant legal constellation, eminently worthy the growing fame of the young Colony. Mr. Ross was appointed a judge of the Court of Admiralty for Pennsylvania, April 14, 1779. In July of the same year he died at Lancaster, in the fiftieth year of his age.

THE DASHING ANTHONY WAYNE.

*A man whose military genius never deserted him—
The hero of Ticonderoga, Brandywine, Germantown, Monmouth, and other sanguinary battles of
the Revolution, portrayed—Stony Point—" Fort
and garrison are ours"—The Pennsylvania General's movements in the memorable campaign
against Cornwallis.*

> "Oh for the swords of former time,
>   Oh for the men who bore them,
>   When armed for right, they stood sublime
>   And tyrants crouched before them?"

AMONG the gallant men who participated in our
Revolutionary struggle, covering themselves
with glory, honestly earning the gratitude of posterity, and disarming the criticism of the historian, was
the distinguished Pennsylvanian, General Anthony
Wayne. From the very incipiency of the war to
its brilliant termination, when peace returned "with
healing on her wings and majesty in her beams,"
his career was that of an honest patriot and a bold,
dashing cavalier, his whole life a thrilling tableau
of peril and glory. The military genius of the man
never deserted him, but gained lustre with age, sparkling brilliantly at Ticonderoga and Brandywine, and
bursting forth in a blaze of glory on the historic and

sanguinary battle-fields of Germantown and Monmouth. Major General Anthony Wayne was born
at Waynesboro, Chester county, Pa., January 1,
1745. His father was a native of the same county
—an intelligent, thrifty farmer—and for several
years was an honorable member of the Colonial
General Assembly prior to the Revolution. His
grandfather, a fine specimen of the old English gentleman, was a native of Yorkshire, and commanded
a squadron at the battle of the Boyne, shortly after
which engagement he emigrated to America. Anthony received his primary education at Philadelphia, and at the early age of 18 was so proficient
as a land surveyor as to attract the attention of Dr.
Franklin, who selected him to superintend the management of a projected settlement in Nova Scotia,
which position, however, he never accepted.

In 1773 he was returned as a member of the Assembly from his native county, in which position he
proved himself not only an advanced friend of free
institutions, but exhibited considerable talent as a
legislator, the fruition of which was only thwarted
by the startling military developments in which he
subsequently played so conspicuous a part. On all
proper occasions he opposed with consummate ability and tact the encroachments of the mother country upon our reserved rights, and did much towards
shaping the opinion of his native State in relation to
the contemplated outbreak which might burst forth
at any moment from the smouldering Vesuvius of an

excited public sentiment. In 1775 he was married, and settling down on his little estate, was appointed a member of the Committee of Safety, in which sphere he gave considerable attention to military drill and tactics; indeed, all his military education was received in this primitive school. The same year he was authorized to raise a regiment in Chester county, and such was his personal magnetism, combined with his great energy, that the trust was fulfilled in less than two weeks. Soon after, he was detached from his original command and ordered to Canada under General Thompson, where he covered the retreat of the provincial forces at Three Rivers, in which movement General Thompson was taken prisoner, and young Wayne was severely wounded. At Ticonderoga, in 1776, he displayed great courage and skill, and was a special favorite of General Gates, who complimented him on his personal bravery and eminent ability as an engineer. At Brandywine he gave another magnificent exhibition of that matchless courage which is as natural to some men as cowardice is to others, brilliantly and successfully opposing for a long time the progress of the enemy at Chadd's Ford. Public sentiment, fickle as the winds, and oftentimes unreliable as it is excitable, demoralized by the repeated defeats of the National arms, forced the battle of Brandywine at a most unpropitious time. Military authority protested in vain against the conflict, which eventuated in an unfortunate but not discreditable result.

In this engagement the Americans were inferior in numbers, discipline and arms, but not lacking in that thrilling valor which afterwards exhibited itself on so many bloody battle-fields. The ground was bravely fought inch by inch, and although partial defeat was our fate, the rank and file were beguiled with the flattering theory so common under similar circumstances in our late civil war, that the enemy lost as many as ourselves. The American commander-in-chief determined to hazard another battle at the first opportunity, and as a preliminary step, detached General Wayne with his division of braves, with instructions to harrass the foe by every means in his power.

The British troops were drawn up near the old town of Tredyffrin, and Wayne's small force was located about three miles in the rear of their left wing, near the old Paoli tavern. Notwithstanding he had taken all reasonable precautionary measures to warrant comparative safety, about 11 o'clock on the night of September 20th his pickets came flying in, hotly pursued by the British troops under General Gray. The night was fearfully dark, and the American troops were aroused from their peaceful dreams only to meet the fixed bayonets of the ruthless invaders. For a time Wayne and his valiant men fought desperately, but were soon compelled to succumb to superior numbers, and beat a retreat. In a short time he reformed his line a little distance from the original engagement, and found that as a

5

sad result of the midnight surprise he had lost, in an
engagement not lasting over one hour, one hundred
and fifty men killed and wounded. The blighting
tongue of slander, and the freezing envy of the line,
anxious to detract from the rapidly-growing fame
of the intrepid young commander, whose pathway
was already golden with bright promisès of the
future, attempted to hold him responsible for the
unfortunate defeat at Paoli. He at once demanded
a court-martial, which was promptly granted, and,
after a full hearing of the facts, he was honorably
acquitted by the finding that he had done everything
"consistent with the character of an active, brave,
and efficient officer." He lost victory, but not reputation, at the midnight slaughter of Paoli. A chaste,
substantial monument marks the spot where the
brave men fell on the night of September 20, 1777.
Soon afterwards he gained additional fame by his
gallant action at the battle of Germantown, where
he led his men into the very heart of the fight with
an *abandon* almost amounting to positive reckless-
ness, having one horse shot under him, another as
he was mounting him, receiving himself almost at
the same moment wounds in his left foot and left
hand.

Although a valiant warrior in the field, General
Wayne was distinguished in the councils of war for
his great prudence and foresight. Before the battle of Monmouth the only two officers really in favor
of an aggressive movement were the two distin-

guished young Pennsylvania generals, Wayne and Cadwalader. The other American officers were influenced and controlled by the opinions of Baron Steuben and Generals Du Portail and Lee, who vehemently opposed an engagement at the time as hazardous in the extreme. Washington, though warmly attached to these distinguished foreigners, and eminently grateful for their valuable assistance, dissented from their theory in this matter and approved that of Calwalader and Wayne, resulting in an engagement so highly honorable to American arms and valor. Here once more Wayne was conspicuous for the ardor of his attack, as Washington makes mention in his official report to Congress. He says: "Were I to conclude my account of this day's transaction without expressing my obligations to the officers of the army in general, I should do injustice to their merits and violence to my own feelings. They seemed to vie with each other in manifesting their zeal and bravery. The catalogue of those who distinguished themselves is too long to admit of particularizing individuals, but I cannot forbear mentioning Brigadier General Anthony Wayne, whose good conduct and bravery throughout the whole engagement deserves particular commendation." An exceptional reference of this kind from such an impartial and distinguished source is, perhaps, the very highest compliment any man could receive. Perhaps the finest exhibition of combined skill and dash in the eventful life of General Wayne was de-

veloped in the storming of Stony Point, July 15,
1779. Having conceived the design, Washington
prudently and wisely committed its execution to
Wayne, in whom he had unlimited confidence.
Stony Point was a very formidable fort on the Hudson, its base being washed on one side by the waters
of that beautiful river. The other sides were pro-
tected by an extensive morass, over which there was
but a single crossing place. This fine, natural position was surrounded with frowning batteries of artil-
lory, heavy breastworks, and an almost impenetrable
circle of skillfully prepared abattis. To make assurance doubly sure, and render this strong position
perfectly impregnable, three British men-of-war were
in the river below, the guns of which commanded the
entire surroundings of the base of the hill. On the
15th of July General Wayne marched from Sandy
Beach, arriving at 8 P. M. within a short distance
of the fort, where he halted to perfect his preliminary arrangements for the terrific assault. It was
a bold task, but the perilous enterprise was in the
hands of a bold man. At 11 o'clock, at the head of
his column, he commenced the advance, the command having unloaded muskets and fixed bayonets,
intent upon victory or death. The fort was carried
by storm, without the firing of a gun. The garrison consisted of six hundred men. Of these, five
hundred and forty-three were made prisoners, the
balance being killed in the conflict. The intrepid
leader, who always led and never followed, was in

the very centre of the desperate hand-to-hand fight, and, while encouraging the men of Febinger's regiment, of which he had command, was wounded in the head by a musket ball. As he fell, he thought the wound was mortal, and requested of his gallant comrades to be carried forward that he might die within the walls of the fort they had so nobly won. A faint conception of the fierceness of the encounter may be gathered from the fact that of the twenty men detailed as a "forlorn hope" to remove the abattis, seventeen were killed. For his bravery on this occasion, justly considered the most brilliant victory of the whole war, Congress presented General Wayne with a costly gold medal, emblematic of the action. His report of the battle was communicated to his Commander-in-Chief in the following laconic letter:

STONY POINT, July 16, 1779, }
2 o'clock A. M. }

DEAR GENERAL:—The fort and garrison, with Col. Johnson, are ours. The officers and men behaved like men determined to be free.

Yours most sincerely,

ANTHONY WAYNE.

To General Washington.

In 1781 he bore a conspicuous part in the memorable campaign which resulted in the surrender of Cornwallis. The British having made considerable advance in Georgia, Washington dispatched Wayne there to take command and bring matters up to a respectable standard. After a series of sanguinary skirmishes and battles, he brought order out of chaos and established general security within the borders of the whole State. The Georgians were very grateful for his valuable services, and their Legislature gave him a valuable farm, as a slight testimonial of their esteem. Peace being declared, shortly after this he returned to his quiet home in Chester county. In 1789 he was a member of the Pennsylvania Legislature, and a great friend of the Federal Constitution. In 1792 he was appointed to succeed General St. Clair in command of the army engaged against the Indians on our western frontier. He succeeded not only in driving them back, but occupied their territory by a chain of military posts, thus effectually checking all future predatory incursions, and holding the ground as he won it. After a year of rough, dangerous border warfare with an unscrupulous foe, he compelled them to succumb to his iron will and sue for a definite treaty of peace, which he concluded with them. He died, December 14, 1796, aged fifty-one years, at Fort Presque, then a far-off western post on the outskirts of civilization, now the beautiful young city of Erie. Some time afterwards his remains were exhumed by a devoted son, and removed to the quiet borders of his native county, where they were subsequently surmounted by a marble monument of symmetry and beauty, the grateful offering of the Pennsylvania State Society of the Cincinnati. Granite, bronze, or marble never covered the grave of a braver man

than Anthony Wayne of Chester county. He won
and preserved through life the love and esteem of
George Washington. To his great natural military
genius he added the ardent enthusiasm of genuine
patriotism; and whether we view him as a stripling
on the Canadian frontier, or as a bronzed veteran
among the palmettoes of the South, or fighting the
local Revolutionary battles of our own latitude, we
find him one of the most remarkable military men
of Revolutionary times, worthy the gratitude of the
nation, and one of whom every Pennsylvanian may
well be proud.

ARTHUR ST. CLAIR.

W E shall not attempt minutely to delineate the character of General St. Clair. His history is intimately connected with our early Colonial era, and from 1760 to 1812 we find him the recipient of high military and civil positions, the subject of caustic criticism and censure, and, at times, the grand central figure of that popular idolatry which always kneels and worships at the shrine of success. His whole life is an epitome of victories and defeats, wealth and poverty, gilded promises and blasted hopes. Although for half a century intimately identified with the development and progress of Pennsylvania, Arthur St. Clair was not a native of that colony, but was born at Thurso, Caithness, Scotland, in 1734. He was grandson of the Earl of Roslyn, and studied medicine with the celebrated John Hunter. By the death of his mother he inherited a handsome estate, and, abandoning his professional studies, he purchased an Ensigncy in the 60th Foot, May 13, 1757. He came to America with Boscawen's fleet in 1758, and served under Amherst at the capture of Louisburg. He was made a Lieutenant, April 17, 1759, and gained great distinction by his intrepid valor under General Wolfe at Quebec, during the same year. On May 14, 1760, he married Phebe, a daughter of Balthazar Bayard and Mary Bowdoin, a half sister of Governor James Bowdoin. On April 16, 1762, he resigned his commission, and two years after purchased an estate in Ligonier valley, at that time on the very outskirts of civilization in Pennsylvania. Here he permanently located his family, erected large mills, and gave his undivided attention to manufactures and other industrial pursuits. After residing here for several years he was appointed surveyor of the old Cumberland district, and in 1770 was made a member or the proprietary council. In 1771 he was appointed a justice and recorder for Bedford county, and in 1773 received similar appointments for Westmoreland county. In 1775 he was appointed Colonel of militia, and in the fall of that year he accompanied, as Secretary, Commissioners James Wilson, Lewis Morris and Dr. Walker to confer and treat with the Indians at Fort Pitt. On January 3, 1776, he was made a Colonel in the Continental army, with power to raise a regiment to serve in Canada. In six weeks after this authority was granted he was ready with his troops to take the field, and, as Colonel of the 2d Pennsylvania regiment, on March 2, 1776, his gallant command took up their line of march to the northern wilds of Canada. After the disastrous termination of the Three Rivers affair he very materially aided General Sullivan in saving his entire army from capture. He was appointed Brigadier General,

*5

August 9, 1776, and Major General, February 19,
1777. In January, 1776, he resigned numerous civil
offices he had held, and, joining Washington in
November of the same year, he was at once appointed to organize the New Jersey Militia. In
council, on the night of January 2, 1777, he recommended the flank movement which precipitated the
battle of Princeton, in which historic engagement
he rendered material and effective service by pro-
tecting the fords at Assumpink. For a short time
he now officiated as Adjutant General of the army,
and in March succeeded General Gates in command
at Philadelphia. On April 1, 1777, he took command at Ticonderoga. The result of this unfortunate affair is well known to every intelligent reader
of American history. On the night of July 4, 1777,
he was compelled to evacuate the fort, his command
being totally inadequate to its defence. Although
his garrison of 2,000 men was badly equipped, he
was sanguine of holding the post, but the forces of
General Burgoyne having obtained possession of
Sugar Hill, which was improperly fortified, secured
a commanding position, and St. Clair was compelled
to withdraw his forces precipitately, which was done
with a heavy loss. From this date he lost popular
favor as a military leader. Public sentiment was
divided in relation to the matter, but St. Clair never
fully recovered from the disaster of that dull heavy
night at Ticonderoga. He was court-martialed and
officially vindicated. The court met in September,

1778, and declared "that Major General St. Clair is with the highest honor acquitted of the charges against him." Though not officially employed, and being a warm personal friend of General Washington, the latter retained him on his military staff at Brandywine, September 11, 1777. He also assisted General Sullivan in preparing the expedition against the Six Nations, and was one of the commissioners to arrange a cartel with the British at Amboy, March 9, 1780. On August 1st of the same year, he was appointed to command a corps of light infantry in the absence of General Lafayette. He was also a member of the court-martial which condemned Major Andre. He was active in raising and forwarding troops to the South, and in October joined Washington, and participated in the capture of Cornwallis at Yorktown. After the declaration of peace, General St. Clair returned to the State of his adoption, and took up his residence once more amid the wilds of Ligonier. He at once was the recipient of high civil honors. In 1783 he was a member of the Pennsylvania Council of Censors, and was a Delegate to Congress from November 2, 1785, to November 28, 1787. During the latter portion of his term he was elected presiding officer of that highly-distinguished and honorable body. In 1786 he was chosen a member of the American Philosophical Society, and on February 1, 1788, was appointed Governor of the North Western Territory. In January, 1790, he fixed the seat of justice at

Cincinnati; *giving that place its name,* in honor of the Society of which he was the Pennsylvania President in 1783–9. His military career now seemed to brighten temporarily; and on March 4, 1790, he was appointed General-in-Chief of the Army. He shortly after moved against the Indians of the Miami and the Wabash. The proximity of the foe was communicated to General Butler, second in command, but not directly to General St. Clair. At sunrise, on the morning of the 4th, a vigorous attack was made by the Indians, and in spite of St. Clair's heroic efforts, he met with an overwhelming defeat, and lost 600 out of a force of 1,400 men. A committee of investigation, appointed by Congress, completely vindicated him, but the popular jury never did. The memory of Ticonderoga was revived, and his military fame was now irrevocably lost. He resigned his military position, March 5, 1792, and on November 22, 1802, he was removed by President Jefferson from his position as Governor of the Northwestern Territory. He had many friends, and, like all positive men, numerous enemies. He had many virtues, and perhaps some vices, but he was bold, brave and generous, possessing the fine courtesy of a cultivated gentleman, and the blunt dignity of a gallant soldier. After his removal from office, he retired to a small log cabin on the summit of Chestnut Ridge, in Westmoreland county, where he spent the balance of his days in comparative poverty. In 1813 the Legislature of Pennsylva-

nia granted him an annuity of $400, and a short
time prior to his death he received a pension from
the United States Government of sixty dollars per
month. He published a "Narrative of his Campaign in 1791," which excited some attention and
considerable comment. He died at Greensburg,
Pennsylvania, August 31, 1818.

THOS. MIFFLIN, SOLDIER-STATESMAN.

*From the counting-house into the arena of party pol-
itics—A member of the first Congress, Quartermaster
General in the American Army, banished from all
the church privileges of the Friends, and President
of the body to which Washington tendered his resignation as commander of the victorious forces.*

THOMAS MIFFLIN, the soldier-statesman, who
wore with becoming grace and modesty the
passants of a·major-general and the laurels of many
an honorable civil position in our primitive history,
was born in Philadelphia, in 1744. His parents occupied commanding social positions, were Quakers
in their religious faith, scrupulously jealous of their
church tenets, and strict disciplinarians. His early
life was surrounded by those advantages and luxuries incident to all well-regulated households where
religion and culture shed their benign influence.
His education was entrusted to the Rev. Dr. Smith,
provost of the University, a profound scholar and accomplished gentleman. For more than forty years,
indeed, during his whole life, he was connected by
terms of warm friendship and cordial intimacy with
his honored preceptor. Of ardent temperament,
sanguine disposition, and active impulses, young
Mifflin, in very early life, zealously opposed the en-

croaching legislation of the British Parliament upon our reserved rights. His father, intending to make him a merchant, placed him in the counting-room of Mr. William Coleman, one of the leading merchants of Philadelphia at that time, a most estimable man, and an intimate friend and companion of Dr. Franklin. He became restive, however, under the restrictions and limitations of commercial life, and yearned for the excitement of public position, where his nervous ambition could have a wider sphere of operation. When the dark clouds of war hovered over the defenceless and impoverished Colonies, threatening them with the deluge of extermination, although many hearts palpitated with fear, and others succumbed to the potentiality of selfishness, the clarion voice of the ardent, eloquent young Pennsylvanian gave forth no uncertain sound. With the self-reliance of an accomplished athlete, he bounded at once into the arena of party politics, and in 1774 was elected a member of the first Congress. In this position his loyal utterances, always pointed and unequivocal, fairly electrified his auditors by their forcible delivery. All positive men have this redeeming quality—that you always know in great crises just where to find them. Morally considered, the positively bad man is perhaps the inferior of the negatively good one, but both are comparatively useless when great deeds are to be accomplished.

Known mischiefs have their cure, but doubts have none;
And better is despair than fruitless hope mix'd with a killing fear.

Thomas Mifflin was a man of pronounced individuality, and his devotion to a principle was so intense
that neither Church, State, nor social considerations
could prevail to mar his judgment or cripple his
honest convictions. He was among the very first
commissioned officers of the Continental army,
having been appointed Quartermaster-General in
1775. Adhering most consistently to their avowed
principles, his Quaker brethren, astounded at his
warlike proclivities, gave him a ticket-of-leave, and
banished him from all Church privileges. Not
blessed with the heritage of a calm, cool temperament, he became restless under what he considered
the tardy prosecution of the war, and on several occasions was unjustly severe in his strictures on this
point, reflecting bitterly and unwisely on his superior officer, the Commander-in-chief. This, however,
was more an error of the head than the heart, amply
compensated for in the future by the zeal with which
he labored for the good of the general cause, and his
many subsequent exhibitions of kindness to Washington personally. He was President of Congress
at Annapolis, when the the latter tendered his resignation as commander of the American forces.
This interesting event, perhaps the most impressive
and sublime in our national history, occurred on the
23d of December, 1783. All preliminary arrangements had been made by order of Congress, and, in
obedience to the same, the great Commander-in-chief,
the bronzed and victorious warrior, who for eight

yea rs had not slept beneath the roof of his humble home in Virginia, was formally admitted to the Congress of the nation, to sheath his sword and resign his commission. He moved into the audience-chamber of the nation he had saved with that quiet grace and majestic presence for which he was so proverbial, amid the enthusiastic plaudits of the assembled multitude. After he was seated, the President, General Mifflin, of Pennsylvania, politely intimated that they were prepared to receive his communications. In a brief but appropriate speech, delivered with great feeling to a tearful audience, he congratulated them felicitously on the happy termination of the war, and indicated a desire to resign at once into the hands of Congress the important trust committed to him. "I consider it," he eloquently concluded, "an indispensable duty to close this last act of my official life by commending the interests of our dearest country to the protection of Almighty God, and those who have the superintendence of them to His holy keeping. Having now finished the work assigned me, I retire from the theatre of action, and bidding an affectionate farewell to this august body, under whose orders I have so long acted, I here offer my commission, and take my leave of all the emoluments of public life."

He then gracefully stepped forward a few paces, and delivered into the hands of the President his commission and a copy of his address. General Mifflin, who was a brilliant orator, briefly replied, review-

ing in his happiest effort the great career brought
to a close. "The glory of your virtues," he concluded, " will not terminate with your military command ; it will continue to animate the remotest ages.
We join with you in commending the interests of
the country to Almighty God, beseeching Him to
dispose the hearts and minds of its citizens to improve the opportunity afforded them of becoming a
happy and respectable nation. And for you we address to Him our warmest prayers that a life so
beloved may be fostered with all His care, that your
days may be as happy as they have been illustrious,
and that He will finally give you that reward which
this world cannot bestow." General Mifflin asserted
his own true, heroic manhood in his eloquent response on this most memorable occasion. Although
a decided partisan, he never dealt in that coarse
abuse and bitter invective so characteristic of his
political friends at the close of Washington's Presidential career. We are apt to imagine nowadays
that party fealty imperiously demands scurrilous
abuse of an honest opponent, simply because he dif-
fers from us in sentiment or opinion. This license,
which certainly has scope enough in modern politics,
is but a dim shadow of the slimy original in the
period referred to, when Frenau, Bache, Genet, Tom
Paine, and even Jackson and Jefferson, poured forth
such torrents of abuse against the personal and official character of Washington that their reproduction is painful to the historian and distasteful to the

intelligent reader. In 1787 we find the name of Thomas Mifflin affixed to the Federal Constitution, promulgated by the historic convention of which he was so prominent and distinguished a member. In reviewing its deliberations and debates, we find him a leading participant in all the discussions incident to the many grave questions then under considera- tion. His utterances and opinions had great weight, supported as they always were by an irresistible array of facts, and delivered in eloquent style, well calculated to wield immense influence in any organic political body. In October, 1788, he succeeded Dr. Franklin as President of the Supreme Executive Council of Pennsylvania, which position he occupied until October, 1790. He presided over the Consti- tutional Convention which met in September of the same year, and by that body was chosen the first Governor of the Commonwealth of Pennsylvania. He served three terms as Governor, extending from 1790 to 1799. During the insurrection of 1794 he utilized his marked oratorical powers to the great advantage of the nation and the State. His earnest, natural, stirring appeals always met with a hearty response from the masses. The imperfections of the militia laws of Pennsylvania were oftentimes more than compensated for by the personal magnetism and thrilling eloquence of her distinguished Chief Mag- istrate, who was as potential in peace as he was formidable in war. Governor Mifflin died in Lan- caster, Pennsylvania, January 20, 1800, in the fifty-s eventh year of his age. His life was a stormy, eventful one, producing for him many friends, and not a few enemies. Perhaps the only stain resting upon his reputation was his identification with the celebrated "Conway cabal," a politico-military conspiracy to have General Gates supersede General Washington in command of the American army. Governor Mifflin lived long enough after the failure of the enterprise to see his error, and made all the reparation he could consistent with the feelings of an honorable man. His courage and patriotism were undoubted, his statesmanship was of a high order, and his private character was without spot or blemish.

GENERAL WILLIAM IRVINE.

A Zealous Patriot, Judicious Statesman, and Conscientious Executor of all Public Trusts—Scholastic and Literary Attainments of a High Order—The Meetings Preliminary to the Historic Provincial Convention at Philadelphia in July of 1774—With the Army in Canada—An Unsuccessful Attempt to Surprise the Vanguards of the British Forces at Trois Rivieres, &c.

WILLIAM IRVINE was born at Fermanagh, Ireland, November 3, 1741. Possessed of a strong, clear, penetrating mind, admirably balanced, he was a zealous patriot, a judicious statesman, and a conscientious executor of all public trusts committed to his care. His elementary education commenced at a grammar school at Enniskillen, and was completed at the celebrated University of Dublin. His scholastic and literary attainments were of a high order, and, soon after graduating, he adopted the profession of medicine, which he studied earnestly for several years in the office of the celebrated Dr. Cleghorn. He was soon appointed surgeon on board a man-of-war, and honorably served in that capacity during part of the war of 1756–63 between Great Britain and France. On the declaration of peace in 1763 he emigrated to the United States, and in 1764, attracted by the number and character of his countrymen who had settled along the southern border of Pennsylvania, he located in Carlisle. Here, by superior professional skill and urbane manners, he soon commanded public confidence and secured a large and lucrative practice. He remained at Carlisle ten years, and deserted his successful professional field only at the beginning of our Revolutionary difficulties, his sympathies and feelings being strongly enlisted from the first in favor of the struggling Colonies. Political controversies at that time were particularly bitter and acrimonious in Pennsylvania, requiring combined tact and prudence to promote harmony in the solution of grave colonial and national questions. Great wisdom and adroit statesmanship were in constant requisition to counteract the evil results arising from certain peculiar conscientious scruples which disaffected several of the religious sects; national prejudices, inseparable from a population of mixed habits, languages, and nationalities; and lastly, proprietary influence, which, through the multiplied channels of relatives, agents, and a whole army of subordinate officials, permeated the entire Colony, addressing itself alternately to the hopes and fears of the community. In such an unpromising crisis as this Mr. Irvine, by his sterling worth and judicious conservatism, contributed no little to pilot his adopted State through her political straits into an honorable harbor. Impelled by an honest love of State and country, and in order to consummate some specific and decisive measures, a preliminary meeting of distinguished gentlemen from various points in Pennsylvania convened at Philadelphia, June 18, 1774. Other meetings of a like character were held simultaneously in the different counties of the Colony, eventuating in the historic Provincial Convention which met in Philadelphia on July 15 of the same year. This latter body recommended a general Congress, denounced the Boston Port Bill as unconstitutional, and declared their willingness and determination to make any sacrifice necessary for the vindication and support of American rights. Mr. Irvine was a representative from Carlisle in this convention until January 10, 1776, at which time he was authorized by Congress to organize and command a regiment of the Pennsylvania Line. The appointee was a man of rapid movements and ripe executive capacity, and, in less than five months from the date of his original instructions, raised, clothed, and equipped the 6th Battalion of State troops, and was at once ordered with his command to join the army in Canada. He immediately marched to the mouth of the Sorrel river, and on June 10, 1776, united with General Thompson's brigade in an unsuccessful attempt to surprise the vanguard of the British forces stationed at Trois Rivieres. In this gallant but unfortunate enterprise the commanding general, Colonel Irvine, and about two hundred subordinate officers and privates, who constituted the very head and front of the assaulting party, were captured and promptly forwarded to Quebec. Colonel Irvine was released on parole, August 3, and, returning home, made every possible effort to secure an exchange, but owing to some misunderstanding between the two governments or their agents, this was not accomplished until May 6, 1778, a period of almost two years. Immediately after his exchange he rejoined the army, and resumed command of his gallant old regiment. On May 12, 1779, he was appointed a brigadier-general, and was assigned to command the 2d Brigade of the Pennsylvania Line, a corps of great and merited distinction. In July, of the same year, he was a member of the court-martial that tried General Charles Lee. He was also selected as one of the members of a court-martial to try General Arnold, but was objected to by that officer. General Irvine commanded his brigade in the unsuccessful attack of General Wayne, at Bull's Ferry, July 21–22, 1780, his command battling with a fiery heroism on that memorable occasion. He continued in charge of his fighting brigade until the fall of 1781, when he was detached to assume command at Pittsburgh, in defence of the Northwestern frontier, then menaced by a combined British and Indian invasion. He continued to discharge the onerous duties of his responsible position until October 1, 1783, some time after hostilities had terminated. After eight years of sanguinary and

doubtful war, the bright sunlight of a joyous peace
streamed through the dark, murky clouds on an impoverished and bankrupt infant Republic.

"Were half the power that fills the world with terror,
Were half the wealth bestowed on camps and courts,
Given to redeem the human mind from error,
There were no need of arsenals and forts."

The appoinment of General Irvine to the command of the Pittsburgh district was a grateful tribute to his sound judgment and executive ability.
The elements he had to control were inharmonious
and almost revolutionary. The frontier volunteer
forces had been treated shabbily in regard to their
pay, clothing, and even their subsistence. This was
one prolific element of discord, and a very dangerous one. In addition, a bitter controversy was going
on between the States of Virginia and Pennsylvania
in relation to certain boundary lines, and this difficulty was gradually assuming alarming proportions,
exciting bad blood, and threatening the most disastrous consequences. Indian difficulties were also
numerous and complicated, and that general lawless-
ness and mobocracy so characteristic of all border
life was rampant and almost unmanageable. All
these combined drawbacks, amply sufficient to stifle
the efforts of ordinary administrative ability, were
manipulated and controlled by General Irvine with
consummate prudence and great skill, and his almost
superhuman efforts were fruitful in good, practical
results.

In 1786, at the request of the Pennsylvania troops,
6

he was appointed by the State authorities an agent under "an act for directing the mode of distributing the donation lands promised to the troops of the Commonwealth," the duties of which delicate position he discharged with honorable fidelity and impartiality. About this time his suggestive mind indicated to the ruling powers of the State the great importance of acquiring by purchase from the United States a small tract of land ceded by the State of New York, and which, from its peculiar shape, was called the *Triangle*, thus giving to Pennsylvania an outlet on Lake Erie. In 1787 he took his seat as a member of Congress under the Confederation, and was associated with Hayne, of South Carolina, and Gilman, of New Hampshire, as a committee to adjust and settle between the several States certain financial difficulties created by the war. These were becoming quite complicated, and even at that early day were begetting sectional feelings and local prejudices, threatening disintegration, perhaps domestic revolutions. Through the instrumentality of this judiciously-selected committee, all conflicting claims were compromised and harmonized on a basis satisfactory to all the claimants, and the tottering infant Republic fast assumed the full proportions of a well-developed manhood. General Irvine was subsequently a member of the first State Convention to revise the constitution of Pennsylvania. As indicating the strong anti-monarchical feeling of that period, this grave Convention stripped the executive department of the State government of almost all its powers, privileges, and patronage. As the natural sequence of such a heated and inflammatory course they ran to the other extreme, and gave to the legislative department a fearful excess of power, thus endangering the usefulness and stability they aimed to strengthen and perpetuate. He resumed his seat in Congress in the session of 1793–5. In 1794 he took command of the Pennsylvania troops to quell the "Whiskey Insurrection" in the western counties of the State, where the powers of the National Government were assailed and menaced. In March, 1801, he was appointed by President Jefferson superintendent of military stores in Philadelphia, and during his tenure of office was president of the "State Society of Cincinnati." He died at Philadelphia, July 29, 1804, aged 63. He had two brothers attached to the Revolutionary forces, Captain Andrew Irvine, of Wayne's Brigade, and Dr. Matthew Irvine, of "Lee's Legion." He had four sons subsequently connected with the United States army. In glancing briefly at the salient points in the life of General Irvine, one cannot fail to admire his inflexible integrity and his very great executive ability. His judgment was never led captive by the glamour of speculation, nor was he a worshipper of fine-spun theories. A plain, practical, good man, he had the supreme respect of his superior officers in whatever sphere he was called to act, and what he did for his country and for posterity was always done well.

MAJOR GENERAL MUHLENBERG.

A Name most Intimately and Honorably connected not only with the Colonial but the subsequent History of Pennsylvania—Young Peter as a Jolly High Private in a Crack Regiment of Imperial Dragoons—Ordained for Service in the Church— The Clerical Robes exchanged for the Uniform of a Soldier—His First Campaign in Georgia, South Carolina, &c.

THE name of Muhlenberg is most intimately and honorably identified, not only with the Colonial, but the subsequent history of Pennsylvania. No family within the realm of the Commonwealth can present a more formidable exhibit of actual worth. For almost a century its representative members figured conspicuously in the various spheres of theology, science, and politics. Their name and fame were not the result of a combination of fortuitous circumstances, nor were they reared on the ephemeral base of mere crude wealth. Their leading members were well-educated men, of strong moral stamina and irreproachable integrity. Their immediate ancestor, Henry Melchoir Muhlenberg, D. D., the venerable patriarch of the Lutheran

Church in America, was born in Eimbeck, Hanover, September 6, 1711, and emigrated to America in 1742, as a missionary to Philadelphia. He shortly afterwards removed to the Trappe, Montgomery county, Pa., and there organized the first Lutheran synod of America—that of Pennsylvania. Dr. Muhlenberg was a highly accomplished gentleman of chaste literary taste, a profound theologian, and for twenty years was a valued contributor to the *Hallische Nachrichten*, at Halle, and the various literary and scientific journals of his adopted country.

Gotthilf Henry Ernst Muhlenberg, D. D., a son of Henry Melchoir, was a distinguished scientist, an eloquent pulpit orator, a member of some of the prominent societies of France and Germany, but was better known in this country as a botanist. His chief works in this, his favorite department, were "Catologus Plantarum," "Gramina Americæ Septentrionalis," and "Flora Lancastriensis." He lived in quiet elegance in Lancaster, Pennsylvania. Another son, Frederick Augustus, was a man of fine natural ability, a polished speaker, and a superior presiding officer. He officiated as a minister in New York until the British forces entered that city. He was subsequently a member of the old Congress of 1779–80, member and Speaker of the Pennsylvania Legislature in 1781–4, afterwards State treasurer, and president of the convention that ratified the United States Constitution. He was also a member of Congress from 1789 to 1797, and presiding officer of the First and Third Congresses. His casting vote carried Jay's treaty into effect. Henry A. Muhlenberg, clergyman and statesman, was a son of the Rev. Ernst, and for several years officiated as a clergyman at Reading, Pennsylvania; was in Congress from 1829 to 1838; and was the candidate of the Democratic party in Pennsylvania for Governor in 1835, but was unsuccessful. In 1837 he declined the Secretaryship of the navy, also the mission to Russia, but accepted the position of minister to Austria, which was tendered to him in 1838. Major General Peter Muhlenberg, the eldest of the three sons of Henry Melchoir, was born October 1, 1746, at the Trappe, Montgomery county, Pennsylvania. The three sons were sent to Germany to receive all the advantages of a thorough and complete education. The early theological training which young Peter had received around the hearthstone of his gifted father was likely to prove an injudicious and unremunerative investment. He soon became tired of monotonous classics and German metaphysics, absconded from Halle, and for over a year was a jolly high private in a crack regiment of Imperial dragoons. His fast life, however, was brief, for he soon recrossed the ocean, and returning to the " still waters and green pastures " of the Trappe, received a solid education at home, and was prepared for service in the Swedish Lutheran Church. His denomination deeming Episcopal ordination necessary, he went to England in

1772, with Bishop White, then also a candidate for holy orders, and they were ordained at the same time by the Bishop of London. Returning once more to his native land, he officiated as an Episcopal minister for several years at Woodstock, Virginia. At the inauguration of the Revolution he exchanged his clerical robes for the uniform of a patriot soldier. On entering his pulpit for the last time, he told his parishioners that there was a time for all things—a time to preach and a time to fight —and now was the time to fight. After services he gracefully threw back his clerical robes, displaying a full uniform. He then calmly and deliberately read his commission as colonel, and ordered some drummer boys he held in reserve to beat up for recruits. The whole affair was theatrical and somewhat sensational, but it had a magical effect, and the honest parishioners of Woodstock rallied in large numbers to the standard of the gallant young commander. They formed a prominent element in what was known as the German Regiment, or Eighth Virginia, a corps eminently distinguished during the Revolution for its dash and gallantry. His first campaigns were in Georgia and South Carolina; and his masterly skill and undaunted bravery in their management elicited the highest commendation from General Washington. Indeed, young Muhlenberg was a particular favorite of the Commander-in-Chief, the latter having great confidence in his coolness, decision, and valor. In February,

1777, he was appointed a brigadier-general in the Revolutionary army, and in the autumn of that year actively and valiantly participated in the memorable battles of Brandywine and Germantown. In the campaign of 1778, he was present at Monmouth, doing good service, and in 1779, commanded the reserve at the storming of Stony Point. In 1780, when General Leslie invaded Virginia, Muhlenberg opposed him, holding at that time the chief command. When the subsequent movement was made by Generals Arnold and Phillip, he was attached to the immediate command of Baron Steuben, and when Lord Cornwallis entered Virginia our gallant young Pennsylvanian was next in command to General Lafayette. He was also present at the historic battle of Yorktown, commanding on that occasion the dashing First Brigade of Light Infantry. It has been asserted with some degree of confidence that it was General Muhlenberg who commanded the American storming party at Yorktown, the honor of which position has been attributed by different historiographers of the Revolution to another person. Be this as it may, there is no disputation as to his dauntless courage and the distinguished part he played at the siege of Yorktown. At the termination of the long and eventful war, when its dark shadows were transformed into streaming sunshine, and peace with her olive wand gave safety, strength, and glory to the new-born Republic, our bronzed young hero, who had exchanged the pulpit for the camp, sheathed his trusty sword without a stain of dishonor upon its bright blade. At the disbanding of the forces he wore the *passants* of a major general, and no knight of the olden time, with his shattered lance and splintered spear, was more justly entitled to meritorious recognition and promotion.

Peace being formally announced, General Muhlenberg returned to his native State, and with that remarkable power of adaptation for which Americans are proverbial, deserted the standard of Mars and devoted his energies and talents to the practical matters of quiet civil life. Men of his intellectual calibre, however, are always restive in whatever sphere their lot is cast, and are seldom contented with a reserve position in the midst of exciting events. They yearn "for other worlds to conquer," and are never followers, but always agressive leaders. General Muhlenberg immediately entered into political life, and successively filled several very high and important State and National positions. He was first elected a member of the Supreme Executive Council of the State, and subsequently, in 1785, was chosen Vice-President of the State at the time Benjamin Franklin was President. On the adoption of the Federal Constitution he was elected a member of the First Congress, and was afterwards re-elected a member of the Third and also of the Sixth Congress. In 1797 he was appointed a Presidential elector, and in 1801 was elected United States Sena-

6*

tor to represent the Commonwealth of Pennsylvania. The latter position, however, he resigned in 1802, and was appointed by Mr. Jefferson to the more lucrative, but perhaps less honorable, position of supervisor of revenue for the district of Pennsylvania. In 1805 he was appointed collector of the port of Philadelphia, which position he held at the time of his death, which occurred on the 1st day of October, 1807, in the sixty-second year of his age, at his country seat, near the Schuylkill, in Montgomery county, Pa. General Muhlenberg, like the other leading members of that prominent family, was a strong adherent of the Democratic party, and although a severe partisan and an unflinching personal and political friend of Mr. Jefferson, was as incorruptible in public as he was honest in private life. He discharged his duties well in all the numerous military and political distinctions heaped upon him, and was as firm in the Cabinet as he was reliant in the field.

ANDREW PORTER IN PEACE AND WAR.

A Boy too fond of Books and Figures to be useful in any way, even as an Apprentice—Failures at the Carpenter's Bench and in Agricultural Pursuits— The Man's Army Record—Services in the Marine and Artillery Corps—After the Revolution, &c., &c.

A NDREW PORTER, the subject of the present brief memoir, was born in old Worcester township, Montgomery county, Pa., on the 24th of September, 1743. Gifted by nature with a strong, vigorous intellect, and a clear, discriminating mind, he acquired through life quite an enviable reputation as a scientist, as well as an honorable record as a soldier. His early educational advantages were limited, but, by untiring industry and indomitable energy, he triumphed over all obstacles in his path, and secured a success seldom attained by those who are favored by more auspicious surroundings. His father, Mr. Robert Porter, emigrated to Pennsylvania in early life, and for many years was a respectable farmer of Montgomery county, the possessor of a numerous family and slender revenues. The old gentleman determined to make a carpenter of his son, and to accomplish this placed him in charge of

(131)

a respectable and efficient master-mechanic in the neighborhood. In a few months his employer reported him as entirely unfit for mechanical pursuits, "too fond of books and figures to be useful in any way, even as an apprentice." The young lad had evidently great mathematical talent, and observing a sun-dial in the neighborhood, at once determined to make one like it. He went to an adjacent soapstone quarry, and having selected the proper material, completed a very handsome dial, but in doing so ruined the tools of his worthy employer. This brought his apprenticeship to an inglorious termination, and he was banished from the shop as grossly inefficient and incorrigible. He next turned his attention to quiet agricultural pursuits, succeeding about as well in his new sphere as he did at the carpenter's bench. Sighing for other worlds to conquer, and yearning for the dignity and autocracy of a country pedagogue, his desponding father gave him one more chance. He opened a school in the neighborhood, and the effort was a financial success. In his leisure hours he devoted himself assiduously to the study of mathematics, his favorite pursuit. Hearing that the celebrated Dr. Rittenhouse was spending some time at his country seat, not far distant, young Porter paid him a visit to borrow a work on conic sections. The Doctor, after making some inquiries about his primary education, pleasantly told him he feared he could not comprehend the work he desired to borrow. In the conversation that followed, Dr. Rittenhouse was fairly astounded at the proficiency of his youthful visitor in the abstruse labyrinth of mathematics, and advised him not to bury himself in the country, but go at once and open a mathematical school in Philadelphia. He carried out the suggestion of his learned friend, and, removing to Philadelphia in 1767, opened an English and mathematical school, which he managed and controlled with much reputation and success until 1776. In that memorable and historic year he bade a final adieu to his peaceful and congenial avocation, and went forth to fight the battles of his country. During his long residence in Philadelphia he was an intimate friend of Doctors Rush, Rittenhouse, Ewing, Williamson, and other distinguished scientific men, building for himself in the meanwhile an enviable reputation as a profound mathematician and an accurate astronomer. In 1776 he exchanged his quiet literary life for the eventful developments of a military career, and was immediately commissioned by Congress a captain of marines, and ordered on board the frigate Effingham. At this time his school contained over a hundred pupils, the income from which enabled him to support well his five little children, their mother having recently died. No selfish or pecuniary consideration, however, could restrain him from the post when duty called. Not liking the marine service on account of its circumscribed limits of action, he was soon transferred to the artillery corps, for which, from his

previous education, he was better adapted. He
served in this latter sphere with consummate skill
and bravery until the disbanding of the army, being
promoted to a majority, April 19, 1781, and subsequently to the colonelcy of the 4th Pennsylvania
Artillery. During his military career he participated in the historic battles of Trenton, Princeton,
Brandywine, and Germantown. In the latter action
his command fought with a valor approaching to
desperation, hurling the invaders back

"As waves before a vessel under sail,"

losing fearfully, however, in killed, wounded, and
prisoners. At Trenton he received in person on the
field the warm commendation of General Washington
for his masterly skill and undaunted courage.

In April, 1779, he was detached with his company to join General Clinton's brigade in the operations under General Sullivan against the Indians.
He left the grand park of artillery at Pluckemin,
May 6, 1779, and on the 13th arrived in Albany,
where he joined Clinton, with whom he proceeded to the Mohawk river. The troops were rapidly marched to the headquarters of Otsego Lake,
and it was here that Colonel Porter suggested to
his superior officers the idea of damming the outlet of the Lake to enable the forces to be trans-
ported by boats to Tioga Point, where they were to
meet General Sullivan's army. The experiment was
successful, and a union of forces being consummated,
the battle of August 29, and the subsequent destruc-

tion of Indian towns, cornfields, &c., accomplsihed the main object of the expedition, and the artillery rejoined the army proper, and wintered at Morris- town. When the siege of Yorktown was deter- mined upon, Colonel Porter was ordered to proceed to Philadelphia and superintend the Government laboratory there, at which various kinds of ammu- nition were being prepared for the contemplated siege. With considerable warmth and zeal he pro- tested against being removed from active duty in the field. His objections were silenced, however, by the courteous, plausible arguments of his Com- mander-in-Chief. "You say," he remarked, "that you are desirous of being placed in that situation in which you can render your country the most effi- cient services. Our success depends much on the manner in which our cartridges, bombs, and matches are prepared. The eye of science is required to superintend their preparation; and, if the informa- tion of General Knox, who knows you well and in- timately, is to be depended upon, there is no officer in the army better qualified than yourself for the station I have assigned you."

The grand object of the war having been attain- ed, and his trenchant blade honorably sheathed, Colonel Porter, in 1783, retired to private life. The trustees of the University of Pennsylvania tendered him the position of professor of mathematics in that venerable institution, which he respectfully de- clined. He was subsequently appointed by the

Supreme Executive Council of Pennsylvania a commissioner to run the State boundary lines between
Pennsylvania and the several States of Ohio, Virginia, and New York, a work for which he was
most admirably qualified, and in which he was
materially assisted by Drs. Rittenhouse and Ewing,
Bishop Madison, General Clinton, and other distinguished gentlemen of recognized mathematical and
scientific attainments. In 1788 he retired to his
farm near the place of his nativity, in Montgomery
county, Pa., where he continued to reside until
1809. In 1800 he succeeded Peter Muhlenberg as
Major General of the Pennsylvania Militia, and in
1809 Governor Snyder appointed him Surveyor
General of the State, which position he held until
his decease, November 16, 1813. As Surveyor
General he exhibited great capacity and executive
ability, bringing order out of chaos; the books,
papers, and archives of the office being in a sadly demoralized condition when he assumed control of its
management. During 1812 and the early part of
1813 he declined the situations of Brigadier General
in the United States army, and Secretary of War;
both of which positions were respectfully tendered
him by President Madison. General Porter was a
man of great personal popularity, decided positivism,
and strong prejudices. In stature he was above the
medium size, rather inclined to corpulency, and his
extended army career imparted to him a proud,
military air and manner, which he carried with him

through life. His morals were unexceptionably pure, his friendships warm and sincere, and his enmities severe and acrimonious. Of his sons, the Hon. David R. Porter was Governor of Pennsylvania from 1839 to 1845; the Hon. George B. Porter was Governor of Michigan Territory from 1831 to 1834, and was long recognized as one of its leading business men and Democratic politicians. Another son was the Hon. James Madison Porter, late of Easton, Pa., who was appointed Secretary of War during the Administration of Mr. Tyler, but whose nomination was rejected by the Senate. The latter gentleman was a volunteer in the war of 1812 –14; and a leading member of the Pennsylvania Constitutional Convention of 1838.

GEN. JOSEPH REED, OF NEW JERSEY.

*A Graduate of Princeton College at the age of six-
teen—First a Friend of Reconciliation, and next
a zealous, impetuous Advocate of Unconditional
Separation from the Mother Country—One of the
Famous Committee of Correspondence, soon afterwards President of the State Convention, and then
Member of the Continental Congress.*

A GALLANT compeer of Wayne, Cadwalader,
and Mifflin, aggregating a military representation highly creditable to our Colonial history, was
General Joseph Reed. Born in New Jersey, August
27, 1741, he enjoyed superior facilities for cultivat-
ing his literary tastes, and in 1757, when only sixteen years old, he graduated creditably at Princc-
ton College. His transition from the classic halls of
old "Nassau" to the law-office of Richard Stockton, Esq., was a fortunate and propitious move for
young Reed. Mr. Stockton belonged to an old and
respectable family of New Jersey, was a man of
letters, possessed of superior genius, highly cultivated, a gifted attorney, and an honorable man. In this
position he remained for some two years, pursuing
his legal studies with unremitting energy and zeal.
He afterwards prosecuted his professional education

in England at the Temple. When our Colonial difficulties were inaugurated by the passage of the Stamp
Act, young Reed promptly decided to return to his
native land and identify himself with her very
doubtful future. He married Miss Esther De Bordt,
the daughter of an eminent London merchant, who,
prior to the Revolution, represented the provincial
interests of Massachusetts in that city. On his return to America he settled in Philadelphia, where
he practiced his profession with eminent success,
and took an active part in the stormy military and
political developments of that particular period.

He was an original friend of reconciliation, but
when he discovered that this could not be accomplished without a total sacrifice of everything like
national honor, he abandoned the logic of peaceful
compromise, and soon became a zealous, impetuous
advocate of unconditional separation from the mother
country. At an early age we find him the recipient
of many official positions of honor and trust in his
adopted State and city. In 1774 he was appointed
one of the famous committee of correspondence, soon
afterwards president of the State Convention, and
subsequently a member of the Continental Congress.
At the opening of active military operations he
closed his law-office, forfeited a lucrative practice in
Philadelphia, and started at once for camp at Cam-
bridge, where he was appointed to the honorable
position of aid-de-camp and confidential secretary
to General Washington. Although a volunteer aid,

he exhibited in his new sphere, during the whole of that memorable campaign, signal personal bravery, united with great military genius. His conduct was keenly appreciated by Washington, and in 1776, at the opening of the campaign, on the promotion of General Gates, our gallant young Pennsylvanian, by the special order of Washington, was advanced to the position of Adjutant-General. His local knowledge of the topography of certain portions of New Jersey made him very useful during the campaign, particularly in the skirmish at Trenton and the battle of Princeton. Perhaps with none of his subordinates was Washington personally and socially more intimate than with young Reed. The latter, at the close of this historic and depressing campaign, resigned his position as Adjutant General, and was immediately appointed a general officer, with the view of giving him the entire cavalry command. This scheme, however, was frustrated by a combination of unfortunate circumstances incident to that period of the War, and for which he was in no way responsible. General Reed was as pertinacious in his military as he was indefatigable in his civil duties, and from the entrance of the British forces into Pennsylvania until the close of the campaign, in 1777, he was seldom absent an hour from his post of duty. He participated with great credit in the battle of Germantown, and at Whitemarsh rendered efficient aid to General Potter in the formation of his raw militia lines.

In 1778, he was appointed a member of Congress, and signed the articles of confederation. During this year the three British commissioners, Governor Johnstone, Lord Carlisle, and the Hon. Mr. Eden arrived in this country on a pacific mission. Their object was to secure peace, either by diplomacy or by duplicity. The principal member of the commission, Governor Johnstone, unfortunately descended from the high sphere of his original position, and attempted by indirect bribery to secure advantages he failed to obtain by legitimate treaty. He privately addressed certain letters to Robert Morris, Francis Dana, Henry Laurens, and Joseph Reed, offering them, in cunningly devised terms, great pecuniary advantage and royal preferment if they would consent to certain propositions.

These advances, appealing to cupidity, avarice, and social ambition, were couched in language more becoming the rank and file of the modern Congressional lobby, and unworthy a dignified commission representing the interests of a substantial and venerable monarchy. Indeed, ten thousand pounds sterling were almost directly offered to General Reed, coupled with glittering promises of high civil distinction, if he would co-operate in compelling a speedy submission of the Colonies. He, however, spurned the sordid proposition with merited contempt, declaring, in his memorable language, " *that he was not worth purchasing, but, such as he was, the King of Great Britain was not rich enough to buy him."* The whole affair was referred to Congress, and a resolution was speedily passed by that body, reviewing all the facts, and concluding in view of the same to have no further communication or correspondence with the redoubtable Johnstone. The latter, on his return to England, in open Parliament disclaimed ever having made any improper overtures to Reed or any other American citizen. In consequence of this flat denial Reed soon published a pamphlet giving a minute narration of the whole affair, reiterating and very satisfactorily proving his former statement. This document was extensively circulated in this country and England, exciting much angry comment and discussion.

General Reed was elected in 1778 president of the Supreme Executive Council of Pennsylvania, which position he honorably filled for three successive years, being elected annually. At that time ruthless partisanship was rampant, threatening the destruction of the whole State government. Under his gubernatorial management violent commotions, outbreaks, and almost positive insurrection were common and lamentable occurrences. The destinies of the Colony, however, were in the hands of a leader of clear head, strong arm, and iron nerve, and for his judicious control of these disorganizing elements he received a vote of thanks from the Legislature. During these exciting crises, when skillfully devised arguments and influences were adroitly created and used to cause a defection in the quota of

Pennsylvania, Governor Reed displayed great tact and administrative capacity. With disinterested zeal and firmness of decision commensurate with the importance of the occasion, he strenuously labored to bring the revolters back to their posts of duty and a keen realization of their country's actual danger. His whole career as president of the Colony was charactcrized by marked ability, amid many discouraging and gloomy circumstances. He was positive in his official suggestions and recommendations, was in favor of a total demolition of the proprietary laws, was antagonistic to slavery, and favored a rapid, vigorous prosecution of the war. His knowledge of law was of great advantage to him in the comparatively crude condition of our Colonial government at that time. Indeed, in reviewing in detail the official acts of his State Presidential career we find very much to commend and little to deprecate. The surrounding atmosphere was poisoned by political broils, filled with the barbed arrows of personal spleen, occasioned by a division in public sentiment as to the origin and management of the war. Feuds, cabals, and conspiracies were rife, and required the hand of a skillful manager to soothe and quell them. After the close of his term, Governor Reed cheerfully retired from a position which had caused him much personal trouble and annoyance, and which he accepted only from a sense of positive duty. His military career was more brilliant than is generally supposed. He had three horses shot under him during the war, one at Brandywine, another at the spirited skirmish of Whitemarsh, and still another at the thrilling battle of Monmouth. He participated in numerous engagements in the northern and eastern sections of the country, but fortunately never was wounded. No stronger evidence of his actual worth can be adduced than his intimate, confidential relations during the whole war with such illustrious generals as Washington, Wayne, Greene, Steuben, and Lafayette. The friendship of General Greene for him was particularly marked, and the biographer of that distinguished man says: "Among the many inestimable friends who attached themselves to him during his military career, there was no one whom General Greene prized more, or more justly, than the late Governor Reed of Pennsylvania. It was before this gentleman had immortalized himself by his celebrated reply to the agent of corruption that these two distinguished patriots had begun to feel for each other the sympathy of congenial souls. Mr. Reed had accompanied General Washington to Boston, when he first took command of the American army. There he became acquainted with General Greene, and, as was almost invariably the case with those who became acquainted with him and had hearts to acknowledge his worth, a friendship ensued which lasted through their lives."

By arduous application to his varied civil and military duties General Reed's health was seriously impaired. In 1784 he visited England to recuperate his failing strength, but without the desired effect. He died March 3, 1785, at the very early age of 43. His funeral was largely attended by the citizens of Philadelphia, the President of the Colony, the Executive Council, and the Speaker and members of the General Assembly. In private life he was a man of pure morals, graceful culture, fervent and faithful in all his social and domestic attachments.

He clung to his country through doubt, danger, and distress, until she reached the threshold of permanent security, and will always be remembered as a gallant, faithful young officer of our primitive history, honest, prompt, and manly in the discharge of every official duty.

7

GENERAL JOHN ARMSTRONG, JR.

*Sterling Traits blended with Erratic Positivism—
The Possessor of the Light Accomplishments of a
Society Man coupled with the more Severe Elements
of a Forcible, Elegant Writer, and a Politico-
Statesman of no Mean Pretensions—Aide-de-Camp
to the Gallant Hugh Mercer—On the Staff of
General Gates—The First Civic Office held by
Armstrong, &c.*

THE character of General John Armstrong, Jr.,
presents many points calculated to invoke
criticism and challenge admiration. Many sterling
traits were blended with his erratic positivism, and
for almost half a century he was prominently identified with the leading military and political events
of his country. At times, on the swelling tide of
unbounded success, he was the recipient of high
civil and military positions, and soon after, perhaps,
was submerged many fathoms deep by the fickle
waves of popular favor. He possessed in no ordinary degree what might be termed the light accomplishments of a society man, coupled with the more
severe elements of a forcible, elegant writer, and
was a politico-statesman of no mean pretensions.
General Armstrong was born at Carlisle, Pa., No-

vember 25, 1758, and belonged to a family of strong local influence, marked intellectuality, and high social status. His father, General John Armstrong, Sr., also a native of Carlisle, possessed considerable military genius, and served with great distinction in the French and Indian wars. In 1756, as colonel of the combined provincial forces of Pennsylvania, he headed an expedition against the Indians at Kittanning, Pa., destroyed the entire settlement, and captured large quantities of stores and supplies sent there by the French for the use of their native allies. In return for his successful efforts in this dashing *sortie* the citizens of the corporation of Philadelphia presented him with a vote of thanks, a medal, and a costly silver tea service. He possessed, in a great degree, the confidence of the proprietors of Pennsylvania, and his opinion on Indian affairs was always considered high authority. On March 1, 1776, he was appointed Brigadier-General in the Continental army, and during the long-continuance of hostilities gained an enviable reputation in military circles, doing valiant service in the defence of Fort Moultrie, and also at the battles of Brandywine and Germantown. In the latter engagement he commanded the Pennsylvania militia, having left the army proper, April 4, 1777, on account of some real or imaginary grievance involved in the question of rank, that prolific source of army broils in all ages and in all countries. He served as a member of Congress in the session of 1778–80, and also in 1787–8, never acquiring, however, a very marked reputation as a legislator. General John Armstrong, Jr., the subject of this sketch, while a student at Princeton College, volunteered to serve his country at the early age of eighteen, and forthwith enrolled himself as a member of Potter's Pennsylvania Regiment. Shortly after his enlistment he was appointed aide-de-camp to the gallant General Hugh Mercer, the latter officer having served with distinction under the young appointee's father at the battle of Kittanning, in 1756, to which we have briefly alluded. At that period General Mercer was a citizen of Pennsylvania, although he was a native of Aberdeen, Scotland, having served as a surgeon in the memorable battle of Culloden. For his good deeds at Kittanning, Philadelphia presented him, also, with a gold medal. In 1763 he removed to Fredericksburg, Virginia, where he practiced his profession with great success until the inauguration of the Revolution. It was on the staff of this distinguished gentleman and soldier that young Armstrong initiated his military career, and it was in the arms of his faithful young aide-de-camp that the gallant Hugh Mercer fell, mortally wounded, on the fatal morning of January 3, 1777, near Stony Brook, adjacent to Princeton, N. J. Mercer survived his wounds about one week, and was buried in Princeton, his remains being subsequently removed for re-interment to Philadelphia. Armstrong at this time was only 19 years old, and incidentally was thrown into company with the distinguished General Gates, who was so pleased with the vivacious manner and captivating conversational powers of the young lad that he promptly invited him to become a member of his military family, which position was readily accepted. He continued on the staff of General Gates, with the rank of major, until the close of the war, and was always a warm personal friend and devoted admirer of his illustrious chief. On the termination of hostilities, the grand result was marred in part by the very great dissatisfaction exhibited by honorably-discharged officers and men on account of the non-payment of arrears justly due them for services rendered in the field. The original spark of complaint was soon fanned into a threatening blaze, and required careful management to prevent its becoming most destructive and disastrous. The oversight in securing the proper kind of legislation was as much perhaps the result of Congressional neglect and carelessness as anything else; but no logic could quell the angry passions of the excited complainants, whose imperious demands were fast becoming dangerous and revolutionary. At this critical moment young Armstrong became a sort of representative of the disorganizers, and, at the request of several officers of high rank, he prepared the celebrated warlike manifesto known as the "Newburg Letters," which created at the time a profound sensation in official circles, and threatened to produce much mischief. They were written with vigor and ability, were inflammatory and impracticable in spirit, and, while they were approved by a limited few, were very generally condemned by the best men of the period. Washington interposed by a counter-address, couched in the plain language of patriotism and common sense, thus effectually correcting public sentiment and re-establishing public confidence. The first civil office held by Gen. Armstrong was that of Secretary of Pennsylvania, during the administration of Dr. Benjamin Franklin; and some time afterwards he became a member of the Old Congress. In 1789 he married a sister of Chancellor Livingston, of New York, a charming and cultivated lady, identified with the most refined circles of metropolitan society. He retired to an extensive landed estate in Duchess county, New York, where for several years he lived in quiet elegance, ostensibly an agriculturist, but in reality devoting the bulk of his time to literary and scientific pursuits. In 1800 he was elected a United States Senator from the State of New York, by an almost unanimous vote of both houses of the Legislature. Three years before the expiration of his Senatorial term, President Jefferson appointed him Minister to France, the onerous duties of which position he discharged with eminent ability. During his residence abroad in the latter capacity he also discharged the functions of a separate mission to Spain, for which he never received nor claimed any pecuniary

consideration from his Government. His missio n
to France terminated at his own request in 1810 .
He was appointed Brigadier-General, July 6, 1812,
and was assigned to duty as commander of the District of New York. In 1813–14 he was Secretary
of War, having succeeded Dr. Eustes in that position. In this new and trying sphere at that peculiar period his troubles and difficulties increased an
hundred-fold. He had no confidence whatever in
the Generals appointed by Mr. Madison, and being
self-willed, and somewhat arrogant, was in continuous collision with his military subordinates, and not
unfrequently with the President himself. The enemies he had made, thirty years before, by his fluent,
caustic pen, in his unfortunate " Newburg Letters,"
had not forgotten their wrongs, and massed themselves against their old enemy, determined on his
political and military overthrow. In addition to
this outside organization, his military movements
were not of such a character as to command public
approbation. The total failure of the military operations against Canada, and the capture of Washington City, in August, 1814, by the British, completed
the demolition of the erratic but intellectual Secretary, and his portfolio was soon transferred to other
keeping. As fruits of his literary efforts after his
retirement to private life, he published an able treatise on gardening and agriculture, a review of "General Wilkinson's Memoirs " (in which he handles
the author without gloves), and a two-volume His-

tory of the War of 1812-14. General Armstrong, with all his failings, was a man of very decided ability, and of unquestionable loyalty. His long-continued intimate personal relations with General Gates made him unpopular with the numerous enemies of that gentleman; and his sharp, pungent, personal assaults with his graceful but bitter pen poorly qualified him to run smoothly in what might be termed the popular groove. Notwithstanding all these drawbacks, however, he secured many high civil and military distinctions, the majority of which he filled with signal ability. His daughter was the estimable wife of William B. Astor, Esq., of New York City. General Armstrong died at his country-seat at Red Bank, N. J., April 1, 1843, in his eighty-fifth year.

THE COMMANDER OF GIBSON'S LAMBS.

A Well-known Army Favorite and His Sons in Revolutionary Times—Careers Eventful, Perilous, and Highly Honorable—General John Gibson's Interview with the Mingo Chief, Logan, &c.

THE distinguished brothers, Generals John and George Gibson, were natives of Lancaster, Pennsylvania. The latter was a well-known army favorite in revolutionary times, personally very popular, of genial social qualities, and esteemed by all who knew him for the honorable and generous feelings of his heart. The services rendered by him to his country were neither few nor unimportant. He commenced his career in a large mercantile house in Philadelphia, subsequently making several voyages to the West Indies as a supercargo. Afterwards he retired to Fort Pitt, at that period a frontier post within the jurisdiction of Virginia. He met with but indifferent success in his Western trading operations, and soon after removed to the neighborhood of Carlisle, Cumberland county, Pa., where he engaged in agricultural pursuits, which also proved unfortunate and unremunerative. He then returned once more to Fort Pitt, and organized

7*   (153)

a company of one hundred picked men, with whom he marched to Williamsburg, at that time the seat of government of Virginia. His men were rather a reckless set of customers, possessing that individual independence, hardihood, and desperate daring characteristic of all frontiersmen familiar with danger and removed from the restraints of civilization. They were all sharpshooters, mischievous without being malicious, and during the war were known by the classic appellation of "Gibson's lambs." The career of General George Gibson during the whole term of his military experience was eventful, perilous, and highly honorable. He participated in the leading battles of the Revolution, and after the declaration of peace returned to his farm in Cumberland county. In 1791 he took command of a regiment under Gen. St. Clair, and in the unfortunate defeat of that officer, while leading his men in a fearful bayonet charge, he received a mortal wound. He was a high-toned, honorable man, quite a linguist, and possessed a vast fund of interesting information. He was a humorist of the first water, and the author of several very popular songs, which he sung with incredible effect. One of his sons was John Bannister Gibson, LL. D., born in Carlisle, Pa., November 8, 1780, and who died in Philadelphia, May 3, 1853. He was admitted to the Cumberland county bar in 1803, and practiced successfully in Carlisle and Beaver, Pa., and was appointed Judge of the old Eleventh District, July, 1813. He was appointed to the Supreme Bench of Pennsylvania in 1816, and held the office of Chief-Justice from 1827 to 1851. He was possessed of very superior attainments, and as the fruit of long-continued, severe, and regular training, his mind became so thoroughly imbued with legal principles and maxims, that they seemed to be part and parcel of his very nature. He was the peer and a worthy successor of the Tilghmans, Ingersoll, and Rawle, when the Philadelphia bar was the brilliant exponent of the legal talent of the country. Another son was General George Gibson, who for over forty years administered the Commissary Department of the United States army with commendable fidelity. He served with credit in the war of 1812, and was breveted Major-General, May 30, 1848, for meritorious conduct in the Mexican war. He died in Washington, D. C., September 21, 1861.

General John Gibson was born in Lancaster, Pa., on the 23d of May, 1740. He received a good primary education, and entering the service at the early age of eighteen, made his first military campaign under General Forbes, in the famous expedition which resulted in the acquisition of Fort Du Quesne, Pittsburgh, from the French. He settled at the latter place as an Indian trader in 1763, immediately after the declaration of peace. Shortly after this the war with the Indians was renewed, and Gibson and two companions, while descending the Ohio river in a flat-boat, were overhauled by the savages at the mouth of Beaver Creek. The two companions were burned at the stake, and Gibson's life was preserved by an old squaw, who adopted him in lieu of a favor- ite son, who had recently been killed in battle. He remained several years a captive, during which time he was treated well, and became familiar with the language, habits, manners, customs, and traditions of the Indians. At the termination of hostilities, he settled once more at Fort Pitt. In 1774 he was an important agent in enforcing the Indian treaty inaugurated by Lord Dunmore, and restored nume- rous prisoners to their friends after a captivity of many years. It was on this occasion that the cele- brated Mingo Chief, Logan, delivered his historic speech, Colonel Gibson being the interpreter. As the troops were drawn up in line of battle, and every- thing indicated an immediate and vigorous attack, Gibson was sent forward under a flag of truce, au- thorized to make overtures of peace to the savage enemy.

En route he encountered the tall, robust figure of the bronzed Mingo Chief, a splendid specimen of physical manhood, leaning against a huge oak tree, his piercing eye flashing bold defiance, and his clenched hand and heaving breast indicating a fear- ful battle within. Gibson was his peer in muscular vigor and valorous courage, and as he approached Logan, accosted him familiarly and kindly: "My old friend, how do you do? I am glad to see you." Logan, struggling to conceal his feelings, coldly replied, "I suppose you are," and turned away. With the exception of Logan, all the chiefs assembled in the council, which was immediately held, were unanimously in favor of an immediate peace. During the discussion of the terms and stipulations, Colonel Gibson felt some one plucking the skirt of his *capote*, and, turning around, found Logan standing at his back, his face convulsed with passion, beckoning him to follow. At first he hesitated, but, being well armed and fearless of danger, he concluded to follow, whfle the great Mingo Chief, with noiseless but hurried tread, led the way to a copse of woods some considerable distance from the council. Here they sat down together, and Logan fairly trembled with grief and excitement. He wept like a child, and for some time was so completely overcome by his feelings that he could scarcely utter a syllable. He then rose to his feet with a wild, majestic dignity, paced to and fro for a few moments, and then turning to his solitary auditor, addressed him in eloquent thrilling terms as follows: "I appeal to any white man to say if he ever entered Logan's cabin hungry, and he gave him not meat; if ever he came cold and naked, and he clothed him not. During the course of the last long and bloody war, Logan remained idle in his cabin, an advocate of peace. Such was my love for the whites, that my countrymen pointed as they passed, and said, 'Logan is the friend of white men!' I had even thought to have lived with you, but for the injuries of one man. Colonel Cresap, the last spring, in cold blood, and unprovoked, murdered all the relations of Logan, not even sparing my women and children. There runs not a drop of my blood in the veins of any living creature. This called on me for revenge; I have sought it; I have killed many; I have fully glutted my vengeance: for my country I rejoice at the beams of peace. But do not harbor a thought that mine is the joy of fear. Logan never felt fear. He will not turn his heel, to save his life. Who is there to mourn for Logan? Not one." After the delivery of this speech, the last utterances of a desolate and broken heart, he sat down convulsed with grief. He begged of Colonel Gibson to communicate his sentiments to Lord Dunmore, for the purpose of removing all suspicion of insincerity on the part of the Indians, in consequence of the refusal of a chief of his position to take part in the ratification of the treaty. After making this last request, the bold, brave, stalwart Mingo Chief darted off like an arrow from a bow, and was soon lost in the denseness of the surrounding forest. On the breaking out of the Revolutionary War, General Gibson was appointed to the command of one of the Continental regiments, and served with the army at New York, and in the retreat through New Jersey. During the balance of the war he was employed on the Western frontier, for which, by long experience in Indian warfare, he was admirably qualified. In 1783 he was a mem-

ber of the convention which framed the constitution
of Pennsylvania, and was subsequently an associate
judge of Alleghany county, Pa., and Major-General
of militia. President Jefferson appointed him in
1800 Secretary of the Territory of Indiana, which
position he held until that Territory became an
admitted State in 1816. He died at the residence
of his son-in-law, George Wallace, Esq., at Braddock's Field, Pa., on the 10th of April, 1822, aged
eighty-two, having borne through life the character of a brave soldier and an honest man.

MAJOR-GENERAL JOHN CADWALADER.

The Youthful Commander of "The Silk Stocking Company" in the Revolution—The Reward of Strict Discipline and Military Bearing—A Combination of the Dash of Marion and the Personal Bravery of Mad Anthony Wayne—The Triumph at Trenton—The Struggle at Princeton, &c., &c.

FOR zealous and inflexible adherence to the national cause, coupled with gallant intrepidity as a soldier, few men of the Revolutionary times were the peers of the youthful, chivalric General, John Cadwalader of Pennsylvania. In the periods of doubt, misfortune, and positive disaster with which that era unfortunately abounded, when brave men quailed, and good men were appalled at the threatening shadows of defeat, with its stringent, fearful penalties, young Cadwalader was calm and undismayed, hopeful and determined. He was born in Philadelphia, in 1742, and at the dawn of the Revolution commanded a corps of volunteers in that city, facetiously designated as "the silk stocking company." This fine organization was composed of select young men from the front ranks of Philadelphia society—the very *elite* of the city. The com-

pany was admirably drilled, handsomely clad, and
its aristocratic pretensions in no manner interfered
with its military excellence. Its youthful commander, of handsome martial bearing, and every inch
the soldier, possessed military genius and taste, and
his gallant command did not uselessly expend its
military ardor in gaudy street parades in times of
peace, evaporating into a mysterious oblivion in
times of war. When the tocsin of alarm sounded,
nearly every member of this company promptly responded, and the majority of its members became prominent line and staff officers, doing good practical
work during the Revolution in spite of their gauze
hosiery. Young Cadwalader was soon appointed
colonel of one of the Philadelphia regiments, and by
his strict discipline and military bearing was soon
afterwards appointed brigadier-general, with sole
command of the entire Pennsylvania forces in the
important operations of the historic winter campaign of 1776–7. General Cadwalader combined
the dash of Marion with the personal bravery of
"Mad Anthony Wayne," possessing, moreover, that
calm, philosophic discretion and devotion to rigid
discipline so characteristic of his illustrious proto-
type, his beloved Commander-in-chief. This happy
union of rare elements combined to make him a
most efficient auxiliary to Washington, whose confidence he enjoyed to a very great extent, and whose
staunch personal friend he continued to be through
life. With his hardy, stalwart Pennsylvania troops

General Cadwalader gained laurels worthy of a Wellington in the historic actions of Princeton, Brandywine, Germantown, Monmouth, and on many other memorable battle-fields of the Revolution.

On the evening of December 25, 1776, Washington made arrangements to cross the Delaware river, determined to drop the defensive and attack the British and Hessian troops at Trenton in the very midst of their Christmas festivities. His army was divided into three divisions. One, under General Cadwalader, consisting of some five hundred men, was to cross near Bristol; another, under General Irvine, to cross at the old Trenton Ferry, and secure, if possible, the bridge leading to the town. Both these divisions made herculean efforts to obey instructions, but the condition of the river, owing to the huge masses of ice piled up on the Jersey side, rendered their passage an absolute impossibility, and they were reluctantly compelled to abandon the attempt. The third division, however, under command of Washington, succeeded in crossing the Delaware, after almost superhuman effort, at McKenzie's Ferry, ten miles above Trenton. They found great difficulty in getting their artillery over. Indeed they did not succeed till three o'clock the next morning. This division was sub-divided into two others, commanded respectively by the gallant veterans Sullivan and Greene, having as heroic subordinates Brigadier-Generals Mercer and St. Clair. This military movement eventuated the next day in

the battle of Trenton. Only about forty Hessians
were killed in the engagement, but the aggregate of
the surrender by the enemy was twenty-three officers
and eight hundred and eighty-six men, while our
loss was but two killed—several, however, being
frozen to death. The balance of the troops, num-
bering six hundred, escaped by way of the road
leading to Bordentown. The British having a strong
force at Princeton, only ten miles distant, and in addition a superior force to ours near the Delaware,
Washington deemed it prudent to recross into Pennsylvania, which he did the next day, having in his
custody all his prisoners. Telegraphs, in those days,
were among the undeveloped mysteries of science,
postal facilities were crude and contracted, and cou-
riers uncertain and unreliable. Young Cadwalader,
ambitious for warmer work than assaulting Delaware
river icebergs, and totally ignorant of his commander's return, succeeded at last in crossing the day
after Washington had recrossed, with a force of
some fifteen hundred men. With these he pursued
the panic-stricken enemy to Burlington, harassing
them terribly, and driving them pell-mell into that
ancient borough. Washington sent his Hessian prisoners to Philadelphia, and they were paraded through
Front, Third, Chestnut, and Market streets, amid the
enthusiastic cheers of the general populace, and to
the evident chagrin of some who were not quite so
loyal. This display was made to convince the positive traitors and doubting Thomases that a victory

had actually been gained—a fact they very seriously doubted and certainly did not desire. The
triumph at Trenton occured at a most propitious
time, and seemed like the first wave of the returning tide. Public sentiment was badly demoralized,
confidence crippled, and hope flickering, when the
joyous news of "a victory at Trenton" strengthened
public sentiment, and drove the chronic croakers to
the rear. The brilliant services and intrinsic merits
of young Cadwalader won the gratitude not only of
his native city and State, but of the entire Colonies,
and were especially recognized by Congress in a ten-
der to him of the honorable position of General of
Cavalry. He declined the generous offer, however,
with becoming grace, conscious that he might be
more useful to his country in the sphere he then occupied. Encouraged by success at Trenton and
heavy accessions to his ranks of gallant recruits,
whose lack of temporal comforts was more than compensated by their ardent zeal and patriotic inspiration, Washington concluded to inaugurate an aggressive movement, determined, if possible, to make
a brilliant winter campaign for the recovery of the
whole, or, at least, a great portion, of New Jersey,
which was crushed by the iron heel of an arrogant
foe. Lord Cornwallis held command of the British
forces at Princeton, and this was made the prospec-
tive point of attack. It is an interesting digression
to remember the cordial relations existing, more especially at this time, between the citizens of the

Colonies of Pennsylvania and New Jersey. They seemed like one great brotherhood united by common interests, and forming a powerful patriotic co-partnership in fighting the battles of their common country. Generals Mifflin and Cadwalader, both gallant Pennsylvanians, lay at Bordentown and Crosswicks, with three thousand six hundred raw militia, and were ordered to join Washington on the night of January 1, 1777. The combined army thus reinforced did not number more than five thousand men. The Commander-in-chief determined to make a forced march from the Delaware river to the left flank and to the rear of the enemy at Princeton, their supposed most vulnerable point. On the morning of January 3, "he arrived within a short distance of Princeton, and but for meeting, within a mile or two of the village, some stragglers of the enemy, would have completely surprised Cornwallis and achieved a brilliant victory. Their presence being informally and unfortunately announced, a sharp, bitter fight commenced at once. The rew militia fell back for a moment under the fierce fire of the British troops, and their gallant leader, General Hugh Mercer, fell mortally wounded while endeavoring to rally his broken ranks."

At the critical moment Washington, by one of those magnificent exhibitions of personal bravery which made him so conspicuous on many a battle-field, dashed forward on his foaming steed · and placed himself in front of the shattered line, his horse's head being directly facing the assaulting foe. The effect was electric and instantaneous. Bravery begets bravery, and the Americans, resuming their original position, fought with the wildest desperation. Part of the British forces broke ranks, and fled into the old college building, where their assailants attacked them with artillery, compelling them in less than half an hour to surrender as prisoners of war. In this comparatively brief engagement more than one hundred of the enemy were killed and three hundred taken prisoners. The American loss was light. Colonels Haslet and Potter, two brilliant young officers from Delaware and Pennsylvania, were among the killed. In this battle General Cadwalader displayed his usual personal bravery and skill as a tactician. He was always calm and collected under fire, never losing his presence of mind and self-control. His whole military career was in keeping with his brilliant campaign in New Jersey, affording additional developments of military genius, and his unfeigned love for his country. General Cadwalader's duel with General Conway originated in the love he bore for General Washington, and the corresponding contempt he had for all who waged a personal war against him. He inherited a keen sense of honor, and his spirited opposition to the intrigues of Conway produced the unfortunate collision. General Gates was ambitious, and encouraged these attempts to place him in command at the expense of Washington's well-earned reputation. Bancroft, in speaking of Gates, says "his experience adapted him for good service in bringing the army into order, but he was shallow in his natural endowments and in his military culture." It will be remembered that, in the duel with Cadwalader, Conway was dangerously wounded, and while there was some doubt about his recovery, he wrote to General Washington, acknowledging that he had done him great injustice. At the termination of the war Cadwalader removed to Maryland, where he resided during the balance of his life. He represented his district there as a member of the Assembly for two years. He died at Shrewsbury, his country seat, in Kent county, Maryland, February 10, 1786, in the 44th year of his age. He served his country well, and left an unsullied reputation as a soldier and a gentleman. A zealous friend of his country and her institutions, his enthusiasm in her behalf was not tinctured by bitterness or malevolence towards others who respectfully differed from him. In the private circle he was almost proverbial in his neighborhood for his genial traits, cheerful temper, liberal views, generous hospitality, and unswerving integrity. He belonged to a family long and honorably identified with the civil and military history of Philadelphia and Pennsylvania.

CAPTAIN NICHOLAS BIDDLE, U.S.N.

Hardships Endured by the Young Mariner on a Barren Waste—Midshipman at Twenty Years of Age—Before the Mast on Board the Carcase, of the North Pole Expedition—In the Revolution—Commander of the Andrea Dorea—The Prizes Brought to the Delaware, &c.

THE Biddle family, prominently identified with our early history, were among the first settlers of New Jersey and Pennsylvania, their immediate ancestor, William Biddle, being one of the early proprietors of the former estate. Charles Biddle, father of the somewhat celebrated financier, Nicholas Biddle, and brother of the subject of this article, was an ardent patriot in the Revolution, and under the Constitution of 1776 was Vice-President of the Commonwealth, when Franklin was President. Another brother, Edward Biddle, served as a captain in the war of 1756, and was a member of the first Congress in 1774, while another brother, James, prior to the Revolution, held the office of deputy judge of the Admiralty, being subsequently appointed judge of the First Judicial District.

Captain Nicholas Biddle, the youngest brother of this distinguished household, a man of marked military genius and intrepid gallantry, was born in Philadelphia, September 10, 1750. From early childhood he manifested a decided partiality for the sea, and in 1764, being then but fourteen years of age, he made a voyage to Quebec. In 1765 he sailed from Philadelphia for the West Indies. The vessel left the Bay of Honduras in December of that year, bound to Antigua, and on January 2d, during a heavy gale, was cast on a shoal called the Northern Triangles. The crew remained for several days upon the wreck, when they were compelled to take to their yawl, the long-boat having been lost, and with great difficulty succeeded in landing on one of the small uninhabited islands a short distance from the reef on which they struck.

With a scanty larder, secured from the wreck, and a disabled yawl, the condition of the shipwrecked crew was desperate. The small boat was refitted, and lots drawn to determine who should remain on the dreary island. Young Biddle was one of four doomed to stay, and for two months he and his companions suffered great privations and extreme hardships on this barren waste. This was pretty severe practical nautical experience for a delicate young lad of fifteen, reared amid the comforts of a luxurious home in the city of Philadelphia. During his two months of exile here his health was materially impaired by scanty and inferior supplies

8

of provisions and water. Such an experience would have crippled the ambition of any ordinary young man; but not so with our hero. In ten days after his return to Philadelphia he sailed for Liverpool, and in several subsequent European voyages acquired a very thorough knowledge of practical seamanship. In 1770, when twenty years of age, he served as a midshipman on an English vessel commanded by Captain Sterling, brother-in-law of Mr. Thomas Willing, a well-remembered, public-spirited citizen of Philadelphia. He shipped on this vessel in anticipation of a threatened war between Great Britain and Spain about the Falkland Islands, and, that difficulty being happily adjusted, he yearned for a life of more exciting activity. In 1773 a North Pole expedition was inaugurated under the auspices of the Royal Society; and two vessels, the Race Horse and Carcase, were fitted out under command of Lord Mulgrave.

Such an expedition, with its perils, dangers, and romance, had special attraction for such an adventurous, dashing spirit as our young American, and he pleaded with all the eloquence of a Cicero to be released from his engagement with his kind friend, Captain Sterling. His appeals were futile, but the temptation to go was irresistible, and he flung aside the gaudy uniform of a British midshipman and entered on board the Carcase as a private sailor before the mast. The particulars of this historic expedition are well known by scientific men, the intrepid navigators having penetrated as far as the latitude of 81 deg. 39 min., often locked up for weeks in the huge mountains of ice. In this same expedition young Horatio, afterwards Lord Nelson, the greatest of Britain's admirals, served, and was a warm personal friend of young Biddle. After certain developments in his native land, clearly indicating a rupture between England and America, our youthful wanderer repaired without delay to the standard of his country. On his return to his native city he was appointed to the command of the Camden galley, fitted for the defence of the Delaware. This service was too inactive for one of his ardent temperament, and he was soon afterwards appointed commander of the good ship Andrea Dorea, a brig of 14 guns and 130 men, attached to the fleet under Commodore Hopkins preparing for an expedition against New Providence. Paul Jones, afterwards so distinguished in our naval history, was a young lieutenant attached to the same command. Writing from off the Capes to his brother, Judge Biddle, he says: "I know not what may be our fate; be it, however, what it may, you may rest assured I will never cause a blush in the cheeks of my friends and countrymen." On the arrival of the fleet at New Providence, that place surrendered without opposition. After refitting at the latter port, Captain Biddle received orders to proceed off the Banks of Newfoundland, to intercept transports and storeships bound for Boston. *En route* he captured

two ships from Scotland, with four hundred High-
land troops on board, bound for Boston. He was
eminently successful in capturing other prizes, and
when he arrived in the Delaware he had but five of
his original crew, the rest having been distributed
among the captured vessels. In the fall of 1776
Captain Biddle was appointed to the command of
the Randolph, a frigate of thirty-two guns, and
sailed from Philadelphia February, 1777. A heavy
gale carried away all her masts, and she entered
Charleston habor in a shattered and disabled condition. After refitting at Charleston as speedily as
possible, he sailed on a cruise, and within one week
returned to port with four valuable prizes. His
spirit and success were keenly appreciated by the
Charlestonians, and in a short time a fleet was tendered him, comprising the ship General Moultrie,
and the brigs Fair America, Polly, and Notre Dame.
A detachment of fifty men from the First Regiment
of South Carolina Continental Infantry was ordered
to act as marines on board of the Randolph. The
honorable, amiable, and professional conduct and
valor of the young commander inspired general
confidence in the whole corps, and gave great promise of a brilliant future. Finding that the enemy's
ships had left the coast, the fleet proceeded to the
West Indies, and cruised for several days in the
latitude of Barbadoes. On the night of the 7th of
March, 1778, the brief but brilliant career of this
gallant young naval hero was brought to a sad close

in a fierce engagement of the Randolph with the British ship Yarmouth, of sixty-four guns, commanded by Captain Vincent. At the very beginning of the fierce conflict Captain Biddle was injured in the thigh, and was supposed to be mortally wounded. He soon rallied, however, and ordered a chair to be brought to the forward deck, in which he took a seat and issued his orders with coolness and precision, amid the blaze of battle and the terrific broadsides of the enemy. Mingled with the horrible din of the deadly conflict could be heard the stentorian tones of young Biddle, the warm blood oozing from his fatal wound, encouraging his men "to stand to their guns." The battle lasted only twenty minutes, when the Randolph blew up, and of her gallant crew of three hundred and fifteen American tars only four remained to tell the story. Thus prematurely fell, at the very early age of 27, as gallant a young naval hero as ever trod a quarter-deck. Brave to a fault, and consummately skilled in his profession, no danger, real or imaginary, could shake his firmness or disturb his mental equipoise. Although a strict disciplinarian, he tempered his authority with so much humanity and affability that his orders were always executed with cheerfulness and alacrity. Fenimore Cooper, in his Naval History, speaks of him thus: "Ardent, ambitious, fearless, intelligent, and persevering, he had all the qualities of a great naval captain; and although possessing some local family influence, he rose to the station he filled at so early an age by personal merit. His loss was greatly regretted in the midst of the excitement and vicissitudes of a revolution, and can scarcely be appreciated by those who do not understand the influence that such a character can influence on a small infant service." Ramsey, the historian, truthfully says: " Captain Biddle, who perished on board the Randolph, was universally lamented. He was in the prime of life, and had excited high expectations of future usefulness to his country, as a bold and skillful naval officer."

At the termination of his cruise he was to have married an accomplished young lady, Miss Elizabeth Elliott Baker, daughter of Mr. Thomas Bohun Baker, of Charleston, S. C. He liberally remembered her in his will by bequeathing to her the munificent sum of twenty-five thousand pounds. Captain Biddle was a man of strictly temperate habits, and possessed the crowning virtue of a sweet Christian character. His genial, winning manners were as attractive in the social circle as his brilliant naval career was jointly creditable to his friends, his State, and his country.

THOMAS McKEAN.

Another of the Leading Men whose Reputation was not Hemmed in by Contracted State Lines, but Belonged to the Nation and the World—Thomas McKean, Jurist, Patriot, and Statesman—Member of the Philadelphia Bar in 1756, Delegate to the Celebrated Stamp-act Congress, Representative in the National Legislature, and Governor of the State.

CHESTER county seems to have been the grand centre of intellectual culture, and the nursery of patriotism during the early history of our country. We have remarked that John Morton and Dr. Hugh Williamson, of North Carolina, were both born in this county, and now we chronicle the same locality as the birthplace of another distinguished Pennsylvanian whose reputation was not hemmed in by contracted State lines, but belonged to the nation and the world. Thomas McKean, jurist, patriot, and statesman, was born in the old township of New London, county of Chester, and province of Pennsylvania, on the nineteenth of March, 1734. His father, Mr. Wm. McKean, was a native of Ireland, and shortly after his arrival in this country he settled permanently in New London. The Rev. Dr. Allison, a learned and accomplished scholar at that time, presided over a quite celebrated institution at that place, and at this school young McKean was placed at the very early age of nine years. This old Dr. Allison, we may remark, had an almost national reputation as a successful preceptor, was wonderfully proficient in the classics, and well versed in philosophy, history, and general literature. The leading men of Pennsylvania and the neighboring Colonies, who yearned for solid learning and polite literature generally, had their thirst quenched at the scientific fountain of quaint old Dr. Allison, at New London, Chester county.

After acquiring the elementary basis of a good education, with a fair knowledge of rhetoric, logic, and classics, young McKean registered himself as a law student in the office of a relative of no mean legal reputation, David Finney, Esq., of New Castle, Delaware. Before he attained his majority he was admitted to the bar, and in a very short time secured a large and lucrative practice, and was recognized as one of the most prominent and brilliant young advocates in the Colony of Delaware. In 1756 he was admitted to practice in the courts of the city and county of Philadelphia, and the following year to the bar of the Supreme Court of Pennsylvania. The political career of Mr. McKean began when he was about twenty-eight years of age, and for several years he held successively many local offices of honor and trust; and by his unflagging industry and genuine ability gave significant promise of that great eminence which he subsequently attained. He was a leading member of the celebrated Stamp Act Congress, which met in New York in 1765, to obtain relief of the British Government from a long schedule of grievances under which we suffered, but more particularly those allied to the celebrated Stamp Act. The proceedings of that famous convention have never received the publicity their importance demanded, excepting, of course, the general declaration of rights, appeal to the King, and various petitions to Parliament. A commendable proportion of firmness and boldness characterized the general proceedings of the convention, but throughout all their deliberations there was an unmistakable outcropping of nervous timidity, dubious loyalty, and that non-committal policy which shirks everything with which it comes in contact. The aggressive wing of the body was engineered by the celebrated James Otis, of Boston, and young Thomas McKean of Delaware; and their stirring and thrilling appeals gave forth no uncertain sound. One Timothy Ruggles, of Massachusetts, was elected chairman of the convention by a majority of one vote over his competitor, this same James Otis—one of those peculiar political results which are as unaccountable as they are common. President Ruggles, although a good man in the quiet walks of private life, was not the most reliable loyalist in the

8*

world, and, instead of being an aggressive statesman, was one of trembling tendencies. When the
convention ceased its operations, and the president,
with others, was called upon to sign the proceedings,
and give them official character, he peremptorily refused to affix his name. This produced what in
modern parlance we might term a sensation! Mc-
Kean, who was impulsive and a seeker after truth,
with proper dignity but some warmth demanded of
Timothy his reasons for refusing to sign the petition. This was a bombshell in the camp of the con-
servatives, and after some parleying and much personal embarrassment, Ruggles replied that he refused because he had a right to do so, and to sign these
proceedings "would be doing violence to his conscience." This brought the impetuous McKean to
his feet, who yelled out, "Conscience! Conscience!"
so long and so loud, and in such a strangely modulated
tone, that the chairman became irritable beyond all
measure, and, forgetful of all parliamentary propriety
and dignity, immediately then and there challenged
his youthful assailant to mortal combat. The challenge was no sooner proffered than accepted, but the
timid Ruggles was no more inclined to fight than to
sign the official proceedings, and quietly returned to
Massachusetts only to receive from the Legislature
of that colony a stern rebuke for his vacillating,
timid course as her representative. Ruggles and
Robert Ogden, of New Jersey, were the only two
delegates who refused to sign the petitions. The

latter was subsequently burned in effigy by his indignant constituents, and forced to retire from the Speakership of the General Assembly of that State. Ogden blamed McKean for communicating to the public his action in the matter, and threatened him with a challenge, but very prudently, perhaps, never carried his threat into execution. Mr. McKean removed to Philadelphia in 1774, a short time before the meeting of Congress. The citizens of the counties of New Castle, Sussex, and Kent, in Delaware, still insisted that he should represent them in Congress, and he was accordingly elected as their delegate, and took his seat in that body September 3d, 1774. He acted in that capacity from that date to February 1, 1783. This was said to be the only instance where any one member remained for so long a period in Congress, i. e., from 1774 to the signing of the preliminary peace in 1783, a continuous term of eight and a half years. It is a singular incident in his life that during all this time he was actually a resident of Philadelphia, while at the same time his constituents were residents of another State. In 1777, although, as stated, he was a Congressional Representative of Delaware, he was appointed Chief Justice of Pennsylvania, thus holding high official positions in both States at the same time, and claimed as a citizen by each—a most singular position to occupy, and an anomaly in the history of politics. He received his commission as Chief Justice of Pennsylvania,

July 28, 1778, from the Supreme Executive Council of the State, and most ably discharged the duties of the honorable position for a period of twenty-two years. In 1780, actually oppressed by the weight of official position, he tendered his resignation to the citizens of Delaware as their Congressional Representative. So invaluable, however, were his services, that his Delaware friends declined to accept it, and he was compelled to continue in the position, more from a sense of gratitude and duty than from love of honor or reward. In July, 1781, he was elected President of Congress, but in October of the same year was compelled to relinquish this position because it interfered with the proper exercise of his functions and duties as Chief Justice. Of McKean as a lawyer we may safely say that he was master of that intricate profession. As a contemporary very justly remarked of Tilghman, we may appropriately say of McKean: "He took in at one glance all the beauties of the most obscure and difficult limitations. With him it was intuitive, and he could untie the knots of a contingent remainder or an executive device, as familiarly as he could his garter." Of his career as a judge it is unnecessary for us to comment, for his judicial fame is the common property of the world. Pennsylvania, however much she may have suffered in many instances by irresponsible and unworthy political representation in the councils of the nation, has always been justly proud of her incorruptible and learned judiciary.

Ross, Tilghman, Ingersoll, Rawle, and Bradford, with a host of others, were brilliant stars in the legal firmament of the old Colonial times, and the lustre of the galaxy has not been dimmed by such modern luminaries as Gibson and Black. But the peer of them all was Chief Justice Thos. McKean. A faultless logician, fluent without the least volubility, wonderfully concise, with a naturally logical mind well disciplined by severe and systematic training, he was a most brilliant advocate and attorney. As a judge he had few equals in this or any other land. When he assumed the judicial ermine, the laws of Pennsylvania were crude and unsettled, and it devolved upon him to overcome all these difficulties, and bring order out of comparative chaos. His decisions were remarkably accurate, sometimes quite profound, and always delivered with a grace of diction and perspicuity of language which commend them to the cultivated legal mind. His personal appearance on the bench was a combination of proper affability and great dignity. In 1788 an attempt was made to impeach him as Chief Justice, but it was promptly ignored by the General Assembly, to whom it was referred. Mr. McKean was delegated a member from Philadelphia to the Pennsylvania Convention which met in 1787 to ratify the constitution of the United States, and was a leading spirit of that body. In concluding an eloquent speech in favor of the ratification, he said: "The law, sir, has been my study from my infancy, and my only profession. I have gone through the circle of office in the legislative, judicial, and executive departments of government, and from all my study, observation, and experience, I must declare, that from a full examination and due consideration of this system, it appears to be the very best the world has yet seen."

In 1788 the Legislature of Pennsylvania took preliminary action in relation to calling a convention to revise the State Constitution. This body assembled on the 24th of November, 1789, and here again McKean was a member of great mark and force. In 1799 he was elected Governor of Pennsylvania, his competitor being the able and distinguished jurist, Judge James Ross. McKean was an uncompromising Democrat, and by his great personal and political influence contributed in no small degree to the election of Mr. Jefferson to the Presidency. His gubernatorial career was marked by great ability, and produced beneficial results to the Commonwealth. He was a rigid partisan, well disciplined in tactics, and a devout believer in the old Jeffersonian maxim, that "to the victors belong the spoils." In carrying out his specific views of this theory, his wholesale removal of political opponents from office was unprecedented in our early history, producing very great excitement, and evincing on his part an unjustifiable degree of political asperity. Party spirit, however, in those days ran high on both sides, as was indicated by a series of charges made against Governor McKean by certain influential citizens of the county of Philadelphia, which resulted in having them referred to a committee of the Legislature. This committee reported adversely to the Governor on six different points, including unjustifiable interference on his part with the election of Sheriff in Philadelphia in 1806; an usurpation of authority in the somewhat celebrated case of Joseph Cabrera; violation of the constitution in making certain Philadelphia appointments; allowing his name to be stamped on blank patents, Treasury warrants, and other official papers; and improper overtures in the exciting case of Wm. Duane against the son of the Governor, for what was termed a murderous assault.

The committee, as we have intimated, reported a resolution in favor of the impeachment of the Governor for "high crimes and misdemeanors," but after considerable preliminary skirmishing, the House, on the 27th of January, indefinitely postponed further consideration of the whole matter, and the impulsive but not malicious official was saved from the ignominy of successful impeachment. The next day a formal reply of his to the charges preferred against him was inserted in full on the House Journal, where it remains to this day, and the whole matter thus terminated. In this reply occurs the following passage, which is characteristic of the man: "That I may have erred in judgment, that I may have been mistaken in my general views of

public policy, and that I may have been deceived
by the objects of executive confidence and benevolence, I am not so vain nor so credulous as to deny,
though in the present instance I am still without
the proof and without the belief. But the firm and
fearless position which I take invites the strictest
scrutiny, upon a fair exposition of our constitution
and law, into the sincerity and truth of the general
answer given to my accusers—*that no act of my public life was ever done from a corrupt motive, nor without a deliberate opinion that the act was proper and
lawful in itself!*"

Governor McKean was a bold and fearless advocate of the Declaration of Independence, and, although
he signed his name to the original instrument de-
posited in the office of the Secretary of State, either
through extreme carelessness, or some political leg-
erdemain of an envious rival, his name was omitted
in the official copy published in the journals of Congress. He occupied a high social position in Delaware and in Philadelphia. In the latter place society was peculiarly refined and attractive, particularly during the administration of Washington. His
daughter, a beautiful and accomplished lady, was
one of the reigning belles of the period, and subsequently married the Marquis d'Yrujo, a dashing
young Spaniard who represented the Court of Mad-
rid in this country, and was an attractive feature in
fashionable life years ago. Yrujo was afterwards
quite prominent in Spanish politics, and his son, the

Duke of Sotomayer, born in Philadelphia, afterwards became Prime Minister.

In 1808, having served nine years as Governor of Pennsylvania, McKean returned to private life with the consciousness of a well-earned and honorable reputation. He had many friends and not a few enemies, the common fate of every man in high public office who endeavors to discharge his duties with firmness and impartiality. On the 24th of June, 1817, he was gathered to the generation of his fathers, at the advanced age of 83.

THE POET, FRANCIS HOPKINSON.

Graduate of the Philadelphia College, Successful Advocate at the Bar, Author of "The Battle of the Kegs," Executive Counsellor and Collector of Customs, Representative in Congress, and United States Judge for the District of Pennsylvania.

ALTHOUGH for several years a resident of New Jersey, and one of her Congressional Representatives, Francis Hopkinson was a native of Pennsylvania, and as he spent the greater portion of his life in the latter, may be claimed as the joint property of the two venerable colonies that fought side by side during the stormy times of the Revolution. He was born in Philadelphia, in the year 1737. His father, Mr. Thomas Hopkinson, married a niece of the Bishop of Worcester, and emigrating to this country about 1716, settled in Philadelphia, where he was justly considered a most valuable acquisition to her select society, and filled in that city several important offices under the English Government. He was somewhat of a scientist, and an intimate personal friend of Dr. Benjamin Franklin. The elder Hopkinson claimed credit for several scientific discoveries which were of great practical

utility, and which were highly commended by
Franklin. Attracting the electric fluid by means of
a pointed instead of a blunt instrument, thus avoid-
ing the disagreeable explosion which invariably
took place by the old method, was one of his inven-
tions or discoveries. He died comparatively young,
leaving a large family in sole charge of his widow,
a lady of superior attainments, much self-denial,
great force of character, and a rare combination of
those sweet virtues and gentle traits which develop
the perfectibility of true womanhood. The influence of such a person was not lost upon her family,
especially that son who is the subject of this imperfect sketch; and her noble efforts in his behalf were
crowned with the most satisfactory results. She
lived long enough to see the partial fruition of a
mother's hopes in his graduation at the Philadelphia
College, and his securing an honorable position as a
successful advocate of the Philadelphia bar. His
genius was quick and versatile, and his acquirements
were a singular combination of profound learning
and the lighter accomplishments of what is termed
a fashionable education. He was a man of fine social points—fond of society, quite a musician, a satirist, a humorist, and a poet of no mean pretension.
His poetic talent developed itself in the production
of a number of humorous ballads, which were very
popular at that time. The well known revolutionary song of "The Battle of the Kegs," of which
he was the author, is perhaps a fair specimen of his

somewhat peculiar poetic development. His ver-
sification was fluent and graceful, and he wrote more
to amuse his friends and subserve the glorious cause
he so enthusiastically espoused than to rival Milton
or Gœthe. In thrilling revolutionary times, when
the pulse beats fast and the passions are keenly sensitive, a light, humorous poet is a more important
auxiliary to the public welfare then is generally con-
ceded. Without such an oné the surrounding atmosphere becomes heavy and murky, and the public mind phlegmatic and melancholy. The avocation of this peculiar bard has been supplanted in
modern times by the expressive pencil of the artist,
and a broad cartoon nowadays is oftentimes more
potential than a logical speech of a fortnight's preparation. We would not underrate the poetic status
of Mr. Hopkinson, for in this sphere he was always
recognized as a poet of the people, amusing, instruc-
ting, and inspiring, a broad humorist, and not a vulgar wag, a bitter satirist, with a good motive always
clinging to his barbed arrow. The poetic genius,
equally intensified and much more cultivated, clung
to the family line, and his son, Judge Joseph Hopkinson, is justly celebrated as the author of our national song, "Hail Columbia," favorably known
wherever the English language is spoken.

At the age of twenty-nine, after having secured
an enviable reputation as a brilliant attorney, he
embarked for England to visit the home of his ancestors, and remained abroad two years. At the

expiration of that time he returned to this country, settled in New Jersey, and married Miss Borden, a cultivated and estimable lady of that colony. The royal government recognized his intrinsic merits by appointing him successively executive counsellor and collector of customs. The latter position he forfeited by the intense zeal with which he entered into the discussion of the exciting questions immediately preceding the Revolution. He gained, however, in return, the undivided good-will of all his friends and neighbors, and was shortly afterward selected as a Representative of New Jersey in the Continental Congress of 1776. In that capacity he gave his cordial and cheerful approval to the Declaration of Independence, and voted promptly for its passage.

In 1779 the President of the Colony of Pennsylvania nominated Mr. Hopkinson to fill the judicial vacancy in the Admiralty Court occasioned by the retirement of Judge Ross, and he was unanimously appointed to the same, and for ten years, until the organization of the Federal Government, honorably discharged its important duties.

He was subsequently appointed by General Washington United States Judge for the District of Pennsylvania, in which position he contributed no little to the stability and dignity of the general Government. One leading point in the life of this eminent man is worthy of intelligent commendation. During the continuance of his extended judicial course he conscientiously avoided mingling in party politics. Thus his official ermine was preserved pure and spotless, and his judgment unswayed by the rude elements of coarse partizanship. An independent judiciary, untrammelled by political hopes or fears, is as essential to the welfare of a well-regulated government as oxygen to the atmospheric breath; and it argues a lamentable condition of society, indicative of speedy ruin and decay, when the politician becomes the judge, or the judge the politician. Either will corrupt the fountain, and the stream must become impure.

When the Constitution of the United States was ratified, all the large maritime towns of the country particularly hailed the result with great joy, and grand celebrations in honor of the important event were the order of the day. Perhaps the most imposing demonstration of this kind ever held in the early history of Philadelphia was that of July 4, 1788, in honor of the ratification. This grand pageant and demonstration was planned and managed by Mr. Hopkinson, and was a practical illustration of that taste, tact, loyalty, and executive ability for which he was always so conspicuous. A contemporary thus describes it: "The rising sun was saluted with the ringing of bells and the discharge of cannon. Ten ships along the river in front of the city represented the ten ratifying States, each gaily dressed in flags and streamers with appropriate inscriptions emblazoned in gold. At half-past nine o'clock the grand procession began to move. The Declaration of Independence, the French Alliance, the Definite Treaty of Peace, the Convention of the States, the Constitution, and the New Era were represented by some of the principal citizens in emblematical costumes. The Constitution was personified by a lofty monumental car in the form of an eagle, drawn by six horses. Chief Justice McKean, with Judges Atlee and Rush in their official robes, were seated in this car, bearing the Constitution, framed and fixed upon a staff which was crowned with the cap of liberty, and bore as a legend 'The People,' in golden letters. A carriage drawn by ten white horses supported the model of a Federal edifice, the 'New Roof' of which was upheld by thirteen columns, the three inscribed with the names of the States which had not yet ratified the Constitution being unfinished. The pilots, ship-carpenters, boat-builders, and other trades connected with navigation, surrounding the Federal ship, Union, mounting twenty guns, and with a crew of twenty-five men. A sheet of canvas, tacked along the water line, extended over a light frame, and was painted to represent the sea, concealing the carriage on which the vessel was drawn. The procession, including all the trades, many of which were occupied with their appropriate duties, the military, and the public functionaries, embraced more than five thousand persons; and having traversed the city, it proceeded to Union Green, Bush

Hill, where a crowd of over seventeen thousand was collected to observe the remaining proceedings. While the procession was moving the printers struck off and distributed from their car among the people an inspiring ode which was written by Judge Hopkinson. The entire proceedings were marked by the utmost decorum. The streets and the windows and roofs of houses were crowded with spectators, but there was not an accident or the slightest disturbance of any kind during the day."

Judge Hopkinson died of an apoplectic fit, after an illness of only a few hours, May 8, 1791, aged 53.

In stature he was below the medium height, and his features, although small, did not detract from an exceedingly bright and animated countenance, indicating mirth, benevolence, with sufficient firmness. He was noted for his classical taste and devotion to science, and his collection of rare and valuable books formed one of the very best libraries in the country. He was of a social make, something of a *bon vivant*, a brilliant wit, and, during the visit of Tom Moore to this country in 1787, was perhaps the most intimate friend the gifted poet had in Philadelphia.

"Gray's Ferry," strange to say, was the fashionable resort of the pleasure-loving people of the city, and at a fashionable inn there, patronized by the *elite* of the town, Moore and Hopkinson spent the bulk of their leisure time. One can scarcely realize

that the Gray's Ferry of to-day, with its deep rail-
way-gashes through huge hills of dry white sand,
its puffing engines and greasy brakesmen, could
ever have · been such an attractive spot as has been
painted by the graceful pens of the old Colonial
poets, and indirectly by Tom Moore himself.

9

HON. HUGH WILLIAMSON, LL.D.

PROMINENT among the gifted men of our early history, and particularly conspicuous in the Constitutional Convention which met in the Old State House on the 14th of May, 1787, was Dr. Hugh Williamson, a native of Pennsylvania, but a representative in the convention from North Carolina. This convention, assembled to define the limits of individual liberty and popular sovereignty, claimed in its membership the most brilliant men of the nation. Dr. Williamson was a patriot and a scholar, and the peer of any man who sat in that historic assemblage. Of classical features, with an aquiline nose, soft, but most expressive deep blue eyes, a massive, Websterian forehead, his finely-carved head surmounted with an abundance of dark-brown hair, he added to these fine personal attractions the courteous manners of a Chesterfield, and the solid virtues of a high-toned Christian gentleman. Griswold characterizes him as "a most worthy and excellent man, of much observation and extensive attainments, and an undoubted patriot." He was born in West Nottingham township, Chester county, Pa., December 5, 1735, and from his very earliest childhood gave strong indications of marked intellectuality. In those primitive days one possessed but few of the advantages for securing an education now so uniformly common through the medium of our magnificent system of common schools and numerous well-managed normal and collegiate institutions.

A delicate physical organization, coupled with a somewhat depleted exchequer, instead of dwarfing or crippling the ambition of young Williamson, made him more determined to succeed in those literary pursuits for which he evidently had such a pronounced taste. Always thoughtful, meditative, and profoundly conscientious, he chose theology as his profession, and in a few years, after overcoming almost insuperable difficulties, we find him a licentiate of the Presbytery of Philadelphia. But the young ambassador from a higher court had studied too much, worked too hard, and had overtaxed his system so much, that, to his great regret, he found himself physically unable to assume the duties of the pulpit. His physician demanded a cessation from all mental labor, and with the return of health we find him very closely identified with the current literature of the period and soon recognized as one of the clearest, ablest writers of the day. His various contributions to the scientific and literary publications brought him most conspicuously before the public, and the trustees of the University of Pennsylvania tendered him the position of professor of mathematics in that institution, which he accepted and filled most creditably for several years. Al-

though his fluent, graceful, and loyal pen was not
idle in those days of heated political discussion, he
devoted much of his leisure time, during his connection with the university, to the study of medicine.
With nervous energy and a bold desire to master
his new profession, he resigned his professorship
in the university and availed himself of the celebrated medical schools of London, Edinburgh, and
Utrecht, at which last institution he received his
medical degree and diploma. After making the
Continental tour, and mingling with the *literati* and
savans of Europe, with health somewhat improved,
he returned to Philadelphia, where for several years
he practiced his profession with very great success.
Again, unfortunately for science, his overtaxed and
overworked system compelled him to relinquish his
second profession, causing him great disappointment
and depression. He withdrew for a time from the
excitement of public life in a large city, and spent
a year or two with a favorite sister, who married
Daniel Nevin, Esq., who resided in what was then
termed far-off Western territory, the beautiful Cumberland Valley of to day. Among the bold, grand
scenery of that lovely section of our interior, he
again recuperated his health somewhat, and spent
many happy hours with his friends and kinsmen
there, to whom he was greatly endeared by his
genial, winning ways, courteous bearing, and captivating conversational powers. At that time there
were no railways, nor even canals, in our State, or

indeed in the country; and Dr. Williamson made this trip from Philadelphia to Cumberland Valley in the first carriage that certainly ever was there, and, most probably, the first that ever crossed the Susquehanna river.   Its arrival created quite an excitement among the yeomanry of that mountainous region, and hundreds flocked from a long distance to see the wonder of the day, a plain, substantial, close-covered carriage.   Wearied with the monotony of country life, he re-established himself once more in Philadelphia, then the great commercial, intellectual, and political centre of the country.   He employed himself mainly in literary pursuits and philosophical investigations, and in January, 1769, was appointed, with David Rittenhouse, Dr. Ewing, and Rev. Dr. Smith, provost of the university, on a committee to observe the *transit of Venus*, which occured on the 3d of June of that year, and soon after to observe the *transit of Mercury*, which took place November 9, 1769.   His articles on the Comet and Climatology, in the "American Philosophical Transactions" of 1769 and 1770, were marked by great ability, and produced a most profound sensation.

Having received his academical education at Newark, Del., he took a joint interest in the cause of general education and the success of the old academy where he had spent his early years, and, fortified by a strong endorsement from Gov. John Penn, he sailed in 1773 for the West Indies, and from thence to Europe, to solicit financial aid in behalf of the humble but potent school in Newark. He persevered in this effort under great disadvantages, but with very great success, until the autumn of 1775, when our Colonial difficulties with the mother-country were inaugurated. He was the first to report the destruction of tea at Boston; and on that occasion boldly declared that coercive measures must result in a bloody civil war. Dr. Williamson, while in London, procured the letters of Hutchinson, Oliver, and others, and caused them to be delivered to Dr. Franklin, who sent them to Boston, for which Wedderburne before the Privy Council stigmatized good old Benjamin Franklin as a "thief!" John Adams supposed it was David Hartly, a member of Parliament, but friendly disposed to our country, who caused the important correspondence to be transmitted to Franklin. After the *exposé* of this affair, Williamson, deeming discretion the better part of valor, suddenly left England, and sailed for Holland. On the day after the reception of the news of the Declaration of Independence, regardless of every personal and business consideration, he sailed for his native land. Unwilling to be a mere spectator, he earnestly yearned to be a participant in the stirring scenes then foreshadowed, and which were destined to startle and electrify the world. On his arrival he found the medical corps of the army was filled, but having occasion to visit Newbern, N. C., on important private business, he went at once to the

residence of the Governor of the Province, and tendered his services for any position in which he might
be useful to his country.   When the British took possession of Charleston, South Carolina, a large draft
of military was ordered from North Carolina, for the
defence of South Carolina, and Dr. Williamson was
placed at the head of the medical department.   His
medical knowledge and scientific attainments eminently qualified him for this important position, and
his gentle manners and high-toned Christian character exerted a most wholesome influence on his subordinates.   After the battle of Camden, August 18,
1780, which the Doctor witnessed, he requested
General Caswell, then Governor of the Province, to
give him a flag, that he might attend to the wants of
the North Carolina prisoners.   The General informed him that his duties did not require him to go,
and suggested that he send some of the regimental
surgeons.   He replied, that such of his surgeons, as
he had seen, declined to go, afraid of the consequences; "but," said he, "if I have lived until a flag
that will not protect me I have outlived my country,
and in that case have lived a day too long."   He did
go, however, and remained over two months in the
enemy's camp, rendering good service to the sick
of both armies, where his skill was highly appreciated.   At the close of the war he served as a
representative of Edenton, North Carolina, in the
House of Commons.   Subsequently he was elected
by the Legislature of North Carolina to the Con-

tinental Congress, where he served three years, as
long a term as the law at that time allowed. He
was a member on that memorable occasion, December 23, 1783, when Washington, at Annapolis, Md.,
tendered his commission and claimed the indul-
gence of retiring from the public service. This was
truly one of the most sublime scenes in our national
history perpetuated on canvas by Trumbull, and now
adorning the rotunda of the Capitol at Washington. Prominent in this picture is the fine commanding figure and sweet expressive countenance
of our gallant young Pennsylvanian, Dr. Hugh
Williamson, who perfectly idolized Washington.
In 1787 he was a delegate to the convention which
framed the Constitution of the United States. This
convention assembled at a most critical period of
our country's history, and consisted of fifty-five
members. It may safely be asserted that a more
august and dignified body never assembled, before
or since; men selected from the very front ranks of
society, educated, refined, and, as it were, brimful
of ardent patriotism. Our recent colonial relations
had imparted to our worthy ancestors a certain
courtly dignity and precise formality rarely found
in these degenerate times. The inclined planes of
society had not been subjected to the dead levelling
system of extreme social democracy. The politicians of that day were statesmen, and the public
officials gentlemen, *sans peur et sans reproche.* Dr.
Williamson was a valued member of the conven-

tion, and a most zealous advocate of the new Constitution. In January, 1789, he married Miss Maria Apthorp, one of the reigning belles of New York city, where he went to reside. Here he continued his literary pursuits industriously, writing on various scientific subjects, advocating the famous New York canal system, actively promoting the various philanthropic and literary institutions coming within his sphere; and in 1812 he gave to the world his "History of North Carolina."

After a long life, devoted to the best interests of mankind, Dr. Hugh Williamson died suddenly, in New York city, on the 22d of May, 1819, in the 85th year of his age. Dr. Hosack's "Memoirs of Williamson," in the Transactions of the New York Historical Society, is a cheerful, eloquent tribute to one of the purest patriots and most learned men of the eventful times in which he lived. A Christian, a patriot, a scientist, and a philanthropist, his memory is very dear to many in Pennsylvania, the State of his nativity, and equally revered by his many admirers in North Carolina, the State of his adoption.

9*

JOHN DICKINSON, LL.D.

John Dickinson, LL.D., Elected to the Pennsylvania Assembly in 1764—His " Address to the Committee of Correspondence in Barbadoes "—Deputy to the First Colonial Congress—" Farmer's Letters "— " The Constitutional Power of Great Britain over the Colonies of America," &c.

ONE of the most forcible and elegant writers of our colonial history was the Hon. John Dickinson. As Wayne was a pronounced type of the bold, dashing warrior, and Franklin a model of human wisdom, Dickinson might be termed the great colonial essayist of the period, engrafting on its current literature in highly refined and cultivated language much that was calculated to create, control, and sway the popular mind. He was the son of Judge Samuel Dickinson, of Delaware, and was born in that State, November 13, 1732. He studied law in Philadelphia for several years, completing his course at the Temple, London. Subsequently returning to this country, he commenced the practice of law in Philadelphia, where he met with very marked success. He was elected to the Pennsylvania Assembly in 1764, where he evinced unusual capacity as a legistor, and on all occasions was recognized as a fluent, eloquent debater. Outside of legislative routine, he was favorably known by his numerous publications on the repeated attempts of Great Britain to infringe upon the liberties of the Colonies. His " Address to the Committee of Correspondence in Barbadoes," who had censured the opposition of the northern colonies to the Stamp Act, was an eloquent and dignified tribute to the moral worth and stamina of the colonists. He was a deputy to the first Colonial Congress in 1775, and the principal resolutions on leading questions promulgated by that body were the product of his prolific and graceful pen. In 1767 he published his somewhat celebrated "Farmer's Letters," which were widely circulated and read by all classes. They were reprinted in London, with a preface by Dr. Franklin, inviting the attention of Great Britain to the calm consideration of American "prejudices and errors, if there were such, and hoping the letters would draw forth a satisfactory answer, if they can be answered." They were subsequently, in 1769, republished in Paris. These letters were twelve in number, and written by a supposed "farmer, settled, after a variety of fortunes, near the banks of the river Delaware, in the province of Pennsylvania." They arraign the British Parliament for laying improper duties on glass, paper, &c., and present an array of facts and figures almost irresistibly strong, and which produced a profound impression wherever they were read and examined. In 1774 he published his "Essay on the Constitutional Power of Great Britain over the Colonies of America." The same year he was appointed to the first Continental Congress, and published, among other important State papers, "The Address to the Inhabitants of Quebec," "The Declaration to the Armies," originally adopted by Congress, setting forth the causes and the necessity of taking up arms; which document General Washington directed to be published immediately upon his arrival at the camp before Boston, in July, 1775. He also executed in a masterly manner, and in the finished style of a classical connoisseur, the two petitions to the King, soliciting the royal interposition for an accommodation of differences, on just principles. These petitions were carried in Congress mainly through the instrumentality of Mr. Dickinson, who was strongly in favor of a reconciliation between the two countries, based on constitutional principles. He was a persistent and conscientious advocate of this line of policy, and oftentimes tested severely the patience of his colleagues, the majority of whom thought that the era of petition had passed, and that of positive action should commence at once. Hence, in June, 1776, he openly opposed the Declaration of Independence, deeming decided action at that particular time premature and inexpedient. In this cautious position he was endorsed by many other members of signal ability and genuine patriotism, but their flimsy theories were roughly handled by the thundering eloquence and powerful arguments of John Adams of Massachusetts, and Richard Henry Lee of Virginia, who favored an immediate and unconditional separation from the mother country.

When the question came up in Congress, July 4, the Pennsylvania delegation, consisting of seven members, stood thus: Morton, Franklin, and Wilson for Independence; Willing and Humphreys against it; and Dickinson and Morris, although present, not taking their seats. The unfortunate part which Mr. Dickinson took in this matter occasioned his recall by his constituents, who did not agree with him in his political views. A short time after the decisive step of a declaration had been made, it is a curious fact that John Dickinson, who had openly in the Congress of 1776 opposed its consummation, was the only member of that body who immediately took up arms to face the enemy. Notwithstanding his Congressional seat was filled by another as a sort of merited rebuke to him, his patriotic ardor was not destroyed, for early in 1777 we find him valiantly shouldering his musket and serving as a "high private in the rear rank" under Captain Lewis, in the movements against the British, who had them landed at the head of Elk river. In 1779 he was unanimously sent back to Congress, when he continued a zealous supporter of an aggressive policy on the part of the Government.

The otherwise harmonious symmetry of his acknowledged statesmanship was injured by this unfortunate episode of his life, when his judgment, lacking positivism, "ran the gauntlet of a file of doubts." On his return to Congress in 1779 he wrote his somewhat celebrated "Address to the States." He was President of Pennsylvania from November, 1782, to October, 1785, and was succeeded in this office by the illustrious Dr. Franklin.

In 1787 he was a member of the convention for framing the Federal Constitution, and in 1788 wrote his famous "Fabius" letters, eloquently advocating its adoption. He wrote another series over the same signature in 1797, on "The Relations of the United States with France," which was the last production of his facile, ingenious, and patriotic pen. His political writings were published in two volumes in 1801, and have always commanded a deservedly high reputation among our Colonial historiographers. In 1792 he was an influential member of the convention which framed the constitution of Delaware. He was a man of profound learning and finished conversational powers, and an ardent friend of progressive general education. The venerable "Dickinson College," of Carlisle, Pennsylvania, which he founded and most liberally endowed, perpetuates his name and fame. In private life he was justly esteemed and keenly appreciated for his uprightness and the purity of his morals. In 1770 he married Miss Mary Norris, of Fairhill, Philadelphia county; and their country seat near the city was for many years the abode of generous and refined hospitality. John Adams dined with him in 1774, and notices "the beautiful prospect of the city, the river, and the country, fine gardens, and a very grand library." He also speaks of Dickinson personally as "a very modest man, ingenious, and very agreeable." Their political antagonism a few years afterwards, in 1776, caused Adams to change his opinion somewhat, for he subsequently describes Dickinson as "subject to hectic complaints." . . "He is a shadow, tall, but slender as a reed, pale as ashes. One would think, at first sight, that he could not live a month; yet, upon more attentive inspection, he looks as if the springs of life were strong enough to last many years."

As a specimen of the vigorous, pointed style of Mr. Dickinson, we subjoin the following brief extract from an address of Congress to the several States, dated May 26, 1779, of which he was the acknowledged author: "Fill up your battalions; be prepared in every part to repel the incursions of your enemies; place your several quotas in the Continental Treasury: lend moneys for public uses; sink the omissions of your respective States; provide effectually for expediting the conveyance of supplies for your armies and fleets and for your allies; prevent the produce of the country from being monopolized; effectually superintend the behavior of public officers; diligently promote piety, virtue, brotherly love, learning, frugality, and moderation; and may you be approved before Almighty God worthy of those blessings we devoutly wish you to enjoy." Mr. Dickinson possessed great strength of mind and a wonderful fund of valuable miscellaneous knowledge, which, coupled with his ardent eloquence and cultivated manners, made him an ornament to the social circle and an important acquisition to our colonial legislative halls. His numerous essays, to which we have made brief reference, although not characterized by great brilliancy, were positive and practical, a sort of patriotic literature demanded by the exigencies of the times, and which were eminently productive of much good. Unequivocal in his attachment to his country and her cherished institutions, his patriotic zeal felt no abatement when old age detached him from the active scenes of life and compelled him to seek an honorable retirement from its duties. He died in Wilmington, Delaware, February 15, 1808, at the age of seventy-six.

HONORABLE GOUVERNEUR MORRIS.

A Man Prominently Identified with the Material and Political Developments of Pennsylvania, and among the Leaders in the · United States Constitutional Convention.

GOUVERNEUR MORRIS, Esq., the youngest son of Lewis Morris, was born at Morrisania, near New York City, January, 31, 1752. Although a native of New York State, he was very prominently and honorably identified with the material and political developments of Pennsylvania, resided in Philadelphia for many years, and was a leading member from the latter State in the convention which met to frame the Constitution of the United States. The distinguished financier, Robert Morris, was also a member of this convention, and the two Morrises, although intimate friends and boon companions, were of different families, Robert Morris being of English birth, emigrating to this country when a lad of thirteen years. Gouverneur Morris belonged to a family of marked social distinction in New York, and was favored with superior educational advantages and privileges. In 1768 he graduated at what was then called "King's College," the well-known Columbia College of to-day, and at once entered the law office of the eminent attorney, William Smith, Esq., the historian of the province. He was admitted to the bar in 1771, and at the early age of eighteen wrote a series of newspaper financial articles which attracted considerable attention and gave their youthful author no little reputation. In May, 1775, he was chosen a member of the Provincial Congress from New York, serving ably and zealously in the same body in subsequent years. At this time, being then only twenty-three years of age, he made an interesting report on the mode of issuing paper currency by the Continental Congress, and its leading suggestions were afterward practically adopted. In 1776 he was a prominent member of a committee to draft a constitution for the State of New York, and was a member of Congress during the session of 1777–80. In October, 1777, he took his seat in the Continental Congress, then assembled in the ancient borough of York, Pa., and the following winter he spent at Valley Forge, as one of a committee appointed to examine, in company with the distinguished Commander-in-chief, into the condition of the army at that point. In February, 1779, he was appointed chairman of the committee "to consider the despatches from the American Commissioners abroad, and communications from the French Ministers in the United States," and their able and lucid report formed the basis of the treaty of peace which was afterwards adopted. Young Morris was a voluminous writer, and a steady, hard worker. In 1779 he published a successful pamphlet called "Observations on the American Revolution," which, like all the emanations from his prolific pen, attracted considerable attention. Early in 1780 he removed to Philadelphia, then the recognized metropolitan centre, the abode of quiet elegance and munificent hospitality. Its wealth, then as now, was gleaned from commerce and manufactures, but, being less suddenly acquired and less generally diffused, had that honorable source and that stability of endurance which renders wealth more valuable for the respectability it imparts than as a means of material luxury. Mr. Morris was a valuable acquisition to society circles in Philadelphia, but in May, a few months after his arrival, he was thrown from his carriage, and his leg was so fearfully fractured as to require its immediate amputation. In July, 1781, he was appointed the colleague of his warm personal friend, the brilliant financier, Mr. Robert Morris, and served as his assistant superintendent of finance for three and a half years, evincing in this position superior judgment and great tact. After the close of the Revolution he associated himself with Robert Morris in private commercial pursuits and speculations, which were extensive and remunerative. He also resumed the profession of law in Philadelphia, and soon took high rank as an able advocate and a successful practitioner. In 1787 he purchased from his brother, a lieutenant-general in the British service, the beautiful patrimonial estate at Morrisania. The same year he issued a strong address to the Assembly of Pennsylvania, taking decided ground against the projected abolition of the Bank of North America. He was a delegate from Pennsylvania to the United States Constitutional Convention of 1787, and took a marked and conspicuous part in its grave discussions and deliberations. Indeed, he was one of a committee of five to draft the constitution; and, Mr. Madison as authority, the finish and style of that historic instrument is in a great degree due to the graceful pen and logical mind of Gouverneur Morris. In order to perpetuate stability of government, he favored a Senate for life, and advocated other aggressive theories, some of which were more profound than practical, and were ignored in committee. From 1788 to 1792 he resided chiefly in Paris, engaged in selling American lands, and in other moneyed speculations; and during these years kept a minute diary abounding in interesting statistics and valuable details. In 1791 he was appointed by Washington secret agent of his government to settle the unfulfilled terms of the old treaty, and although he remained in London for some time, his efforts in this peculiar sphere were not crowned with very abundant success. In 1792 he was appointed minister plenipotentiary to France, and during the revolution there exhibited commendable prudence in his official and personal relations, although his sympathies were

not with the more democratic side. He held this
position until October, 1794, when he was recalled
at the request of the French Government. Gracefully relinquishing his diplomatic portfolio, Mr.
Morris travelled in Europe until the autumn of 1798,
and while in Vienna endeavored to effect the libera-
tion of the Marquis Layfayette from his dreary prison
at Olmutz. Becoming surfeited with the attractions
of his continental tour, he returned in 1800 to his
princely estate at Morrisania, and shortly afterwards
was elected by the Legislature of New York to fill
a vacancy in the United States Senate. He served
with considerable distinction in that body until
1803, acting then and ever after with the Federalists.
In the contest, however, between Jefferson and Burr,
although not a pronounced friend of either, he preferred the former. He spent the latter years of
his life in retirement amid his books and friends,
dispensing a liberal hospitality, and maintaining an
extensive correspondence with distinguished men in
Europe and America. Occasionally he would issue
from his quiet sylvan retreat at Morrisania to in-
dulge his literary taste, and in response to the numerous demands for his valuable services, he delivered funeral orations on Washington, Hamilton,
and Governor George Clinton. In 1812 he delivered an able oration before the New York Historical
Society, and shortly afterwards an address on "the
deliverance of Europe from the yoke of military
despotism," the latter production attracting consider-

able attention on account of its original and very peculiar views. In 1816 he delivered one of his characteristic orations on the occasion of his appointment as president of the New York Historical Society. Gouverneur Morris was a chaste, classical writer and a polished speaker—indeed, he was considered by many persons a powerful orator when thoroughly aroused and interested in his subject. His delivery was fluent, and his language choice, but his force was sometimes compromised by his florid style and extreme flights of fancy. He had a most commanding presence, and in person his resemblance to General Washington was so close that he stood as a model of his form to the celebrated sculptor Houdon. He was one of the early and life-long friends of the Erie Canal, and was chairman of its board of commissioners from their first appointment until near the close of his long and useful life. Sometimes in his official and personal relations he was rather arbitrary and overbearing, and never possessed that moral equipoise and self-command so essential to successful statesmanship. Although a *bon vivant*, and a man of the world, there was a religious vein in his composition which developed itself on many occasions. He regarded religious principles as necessary to national independence and peace. "There must be something," he remarked in his declining years, "more to hope for than pleasure, wealth, and power; something more to fear than poverty and pain; something after death, more terrible than death; *there must be religion.* When that ligament is torn, society is disjointed, and its members perish." This final testimony is the more important, as Mr. Jefferson represented that Morris was not a believer in Christianity. As the latter gentleman was not what might be termed good theological authority, his criticism must be accepted *cum grano salis.*

Gouverneur Morris died at Morrisania, N. Y., November 6, 1816, aged 64.

BENJAMIN WEST, OF PENNSYLVANIA.

*A Skillful Artist and an Unflinching Patriot—
The First Picture Painted at the Side of an Old-
fashioned Cradle—What Followed a Proposed Caucus by the Religiously-disposed Quaker Elders—
Four Years of Study in Italy, and the Result, &c.*

THE township of Springfield, Delaware county,
Pennsylvania, is honored as the birthplace of
Benjamin West. Here the great Anglo-American
painter was born, October. 10, 1738, and here for a
score of years he rambled amid the hills and groves
of this now beautiful suburban portion of Philadelphia, quietly laying the foundation work of his
future celebrity. In his humble country home,
surrounded by all the drawbacks incident to our
primitive history, with no armorial ensigns, wealthy
patrons, or paid critics, he labored with an assiduity
worthy his native genius, until he honestly achieved
a world-wide reputation. He was the youngest of
ten children of John West, who married Sarah
Pearson, of good old Quaker stock, his ancestors
having emigrated to this country with William
Penn at the time of his second visit here. Many
of his descendants are respectable, honored residents

of Delaware county. Although at an early age and through a long life he basked in the sunshine of royal favor, having exchanged the simplicity of his rural home for the gorgeous drapery of Windsor Castle, Benjamin West never failed, when necessary, to enunciate his devotion to his native land. Whilst we yield him due homage as a skillful artist, we must also bow with the inspiration of gratitude at the remembrance of his unflinching patriotism, oftentimes severely tested in a social crucible where his personal friends were the sworn enemies of his country. Flattered and lionized in a foreign court, whose great monarchical head was his most liberal friend, he never quibbled nor quailed to king or courtier on any question involving our national honor.

Benjamin West was a natural-born artist, and at the early age of seven, when he had actually never seen a picture, his youthful genius was awakened by the sweet smile of an infant niece he was rocking in an old-fashioned cradle. In a short time, with red and black ink, he produced a lovely picture of the little innocent, which astounded his parents, and was the marvel of the whole neighborhood. His mother, particularly, was delighted with this precocious sign of talent, and her admiration vastly encouraged the boy artist. He was sent to the village school, but made little progress in the usual elementary branches, his whole mind being absorbed in sketches and drawing, and his juvenile

10

portfolio filled with crude pictures of birds, beasts, and reptiles. Some religiously-disposed Quaker elders in the vicinity held a profound caucus about the matter, and after conferring with the father, the latter did all he could to repress his son's artistic ardor, and issued a sort of domestic *pronunciamento* on the sinfulness of his course. All in vain, however, for, as a family tradition relates, the next day he was sent out to plough. His father in a few hours went into the fields to encourage him in his agricultural pursuits, and was surprised and shocked to find the youngster completing a pokeberry etching of a near neighbor, which was so strikingly correct as to make the sedate parent emit a ghastly smile. "Misfortunes never come singly, but in battalions," and the troubles of the elder West were just beginning. Some friendly Indians taught his son how to prepare red and yellow colors, and he pilfered some of his mother's indigo, which completed all the elementary colors of his pallet, the tail of a venerable family cat furnishing him hair for his brushes. The boy was considered incorrigible, and, as a sad compromise, was permitted by his broken-hearted parents to go to Philadelphia to pursue painting as a profession. At the early age of sixteen he started out in the broad world as the architect of his own fortune, and for five years read and studied, observed and practiced, and absorbed all the information he could, in the city of his early adoption. Several of his landscapes, executed on panels, are still preserved at the Hospital in Philadelphia, where his great picture of "Christ Healing the Sick" is also on exhibition. The British Institute presented him with three thousand guineas for this celebrated work of art. The sign at the Bull's Head Tavern, which long hung in Strawberry Alley, was one of his early productions, and was purchased some twenty years ago and taken to England. In 1759 he sailed for Italy, where he spent four years in the studios of the great masters.

He was rather waggish for a Quaker and very fond of a joke. His preceptor was engaged on a celebrated picture, and during a temporary absence of a few minutes was surprised on his return to find a fly on a prominent part of the canvas. His surprise was increased when the fly refused to move, and proved to be a correct imitation of one, by his jolly young American pupil. He removed to London in 1763, where he permanently settled and achieved his great reputation. Two years afterwards he married Miss Shewell, an accomplished young lady of Philadelphia. His whole life was an eventful one, but grandly progressive. When he had made some considerable progress, the result of his Philadelphia advantages, at the early age of seventeen he travelled around in the villages near that city as a portrait painter, and on one of these trips painted for a country gunsmith his first historical picture, "The Death of Socrates." A year or two later he was painting for the first families of

New York and Philadelphia, and it was through
the noble generosity of some of these parties that
he was enabled to go abroad to pursue his studies.
At Rome he was patronized by Lord Grantham,
whose portrait he painted; became the intimate
friend of Mugs, and, as the first American artist
ever seen in Italy, attracted much attention. Here
he painted his "Cimon and Iphigenia," and "An-
gelica and Medora," and was elected a member of
the Academies of Florence, Bologna, and Parma.
Among his early productions at London was the
subject of "Agrippina Landing. at Brundusium
with the Ashes of Germanicus." His theme originated from a conversation at the table of the Arch-
bishop of York, where he was a guest. It attracted the special attention of George III., who was
his steady friend and patron for forty years, during
which time he sketched or painted over 400 pictures. His celebrated picture of "The Death of
General Wolfe," painted in the costume of the
period, contrary to the advice of his most distinguished professional compeers, effected a revolution
in historic art. He painted a series of twenty-eight
religious pictures for King George, most of which
still adorn the walls of Windsor Castle. His most
brilliant productions were "Christ Healing the Sick,"
"Death on the Pale Horse," and the "Battle of La
Hague." His marked recognition by King George
stamped his fame as an artist, and made the latter
his munificent patron. After the battle of Brandy-

wine, several Ministers of the court endeavored to create a breach between the two, representing West as a Whig, or, what was worse, as a rebel.

The King, in conversation with him, endeavored to develop his real sentiments in relation to the colonial difficulties. He succeeded admirably, for West, in very strong language, stated openly and firmly the many wrongs his country had suffered. He rehearsed these with a warmth and eloquence which seemed to captivate his royal listener; and the King, in presence of his Ministers, complimented him for his love of country, and his manly, fearless exhibition of the same. At the foundation of the Royal Academy in 1768, he became a member of it, and succeeded the distinguished Sir Joshua Reynolds as its President. The honor of knighthood tendered him by King George, through the Duke of Gloucester, was respectfully declined. The tinsel and glitter of royalty failed to conquer strong convictions of duty—the Quaker continued true to his principles.

Through his long, varied, and eminently brilliant professional career, Benjamin West was the generous friend, adviser, and patron of young artists. He did all he could to assist them in the tortuous path of fame, and was always ready to consult and confer with and encourage youthful genius. He never assumed that dogmatic air of personal superiority incident to so many men who have rapidly acquired wealth or reputation, but was kind, persuasive, sympathetic, and gentle as a little child. As a painter, he is celebrated for gracefulness of execution and harmony of coloring. Without doubt he stands at the very head of American artists, and was intimately and most honorably identified with the English school in its palmiest days during the last century. He died calmly and sweetly, in London, March 10, 1820, at the age of eighty-one, and was buried with great pomp at St. Paul's Cathedral. What a life of rapid transitions and magnificent triumphs! The peasant boy of Delaware county in the far-off colony of Pennsylvania, with his crude pallet and lean portfolio, developed into the favorite artist of the ruling monarch of England; his fame the property of the world; his life pure, spotless, and blameless, and his death the signal for as grand a funeral pageant as ever crossed the threshold of Old Saint Paul's!

ROBERT FULTON, THE INVENTOR.

The Trial of the Submarine or Plunging Boat in the Harbor of Brest—Subsequent Brilliant Achievements, exciting the Admiration of the Scientific World.

ROBERT FULTON, the great inventor, profound scientist, graceful artist, and skillful engineer, was a native of the humble village of Little Britain, Lancaster county, Pennsylvania. He was of Irish descent, and was born in 1765. In many respects Robert Fulton was a most remarkable man, and to him is unquestionably due the credit of first carrying into successful practice the idea of using steam-power in navigation. It is less than seventy years since he first utilized steam for the propulsion of vessels, and as the result of his wonderful inventive genius the last threescore and ten years have witnessed a complete revolution in the commerce, navigation, and carrying trade of the whole world. This one brilliant achievement has stamped him with a world-wide reputation, richly merited and gratefully yielded. At the age of three years young Fulton lost his father. He received the best education a common country school afforded, occasionally straying off to the few workshops and manufactories of which Lancaster city at that time boasted, taking the greatest interest in everything connected with their machinery. When he was about seventeen years of age he opened a studio in Philadelphia, as a painter of portraits and landscapes. His name appears in the directory of Philadelphia for 1785, as a miniature painter, although his first six months in the city were really spent as an apprentice to a skillful goldsmith. His career as an artist was remarkably successful, and he was patronized by the very *elite* of Philadelphia. At the age of twenty-one he had accumulated sufficient funds to purchase a farm in Washington county, in Western Pennsylvania, which he generously gave to his widowed mother, and upon which she at once located. Some wealthy gentlemen of culture and refinement in Philadelphia, attracted by his talents, advised him to visit Europe and place himself under the care and instruction of his distinguished countryman, Benjamin West, who, at that time, was in the zenith of his professional glory, and an especial favorite of George III. In 1786 young Fulton arrived in London, and was most kindly received by West, under whose tuition he pursued the study of his favorite art for several years. He made brilliant progress in his new sphere, and secured and always retained the admiration and friendship of his talented preceptor. After leaving the studio of West he made an extended tour to examine the treasures of art in the various country residences of the English nobility. He remained in Devonshire two years, where he made the acquaintance of Earl Stanhope and the Duke of Bridgewater, the latter the recognized founder of the canal system of Great Britain. It was undoubtedly at the suggestion of these gentlemen that Fulton bade adieu to the fine arts and turned his attention to mechanics and civil engineering. Lord Stanhope himself was a mechanical projector of no mean pretensions, and he gave some important ideas and suggestions to his skillful and ingenious young American *protegé*. Fulton remained eighteen months in Birmingham, probably in some subordinate capacity in connection with the canal then being constructed near that city. At Birmingham he formed the acquaintance of James Watt, the distinguished mechanician, engineer, and inventor, whose contributions to science have been so elaborate, and, withal, so practical. During his residence here he invented an improved mill for sawing marble, for which he received a vote of thanks and an honorary medal from the British Society for the Promotion of Arts and Commerce. To this period are referred his patented machines for spinning flax and making ropes, and the invention of an excavator for scooping out channels, canals, and aqueducts.

In 1793, being already familiarized with the idea of using steam as a propelling power for boats, he was associated in a project to improve inland navigation. In 1795 he contributed sundry essays to the London *Morning Star*, and the succeeding year published his treatise on the improvement of canal navigation.

19*

At this same period he published a practical, sensible letter to the Governor of his native State, pointing out the manifold advantages of canals over turnpikes, and sent a copy of the same to General Washington, who courteously acknowledged its reception and its many strong points. Having obtained a patent in England for canal improvements, and perhaps overestimating its practical utility, he went to France, determined, if possible, to introduce it to popular favor. In 1797 he took up his residence in Paris, and formed an intimate acquaintance with the Hon. Joel Barlow, the American representative at the French court. The latter gentleman was strongly attached to him, and he remained with Mr. Barlow for seven years, studying the modern languages and the branches of science more directly connected with his profession. At this time he invented a submarine, or plunging-boat, connected with which were bombs and torpedoes, the whole affair aggregating a fearful auxiliary for naval warfare, but a little too far in advance of the age to be fully appreciated. He invited the attention of the French government to his invention, and Bonaparte, then First Consul, appointed Volney, La Place, and Monge as a commission to examine its claims. The experiment was made in the harbor of Brest, in the spring of 1801. The inventor could descend to any depth or rise to the surface, and where no very strong current interfered the boat was quite obedient to her helm while under water.

Fulton remained in the boat, while submerged, for over four hours; but its motion while in this condition was slow and its power to stem a strong current was limited. The French government through its commissioners declined to patronize the American novelty, though they spoke highly of the skill and ingenuity displayed by its inventor. Fulton realized the position he occupied, the prejudice that was excited against him, and the notorious jealousy with which French engineers looked upon all foreign competitors. In addition to his inventive genius Fulton had a full complement of lobby assurance, and stormed every available point in court and committee to have his plans adopted. We verily believe he must have overstepped the grounds of propriety with the grave Napoleon, for at a certain court ball the latter remarked excitedly to ex-Ambassador Livingston, "*Debarrassez moi de ce fou d'Americain*," which remark, though emanating from a Royal source, was more pointed than polite. The condemned "fou d'Americain" subsequently excited the admiration of the scientific world by his brilliant achievements, and reared a shaft of fame more enduring than the dynasty of the Bonapartes. Failing in France, Fulton accepted an invitation from the English Ministry, who also appointed a commission to test the merits of his torpedo. Mr. Pitt was very friendly disposed to the invention, but Lord Melville was strongly opposed, and condemned it as visionary and impracticable. In December, 1806, he returned to New York, where he was supplied with the necessary capital by the Hon. Robt. Livingston, with which he built the celebrated "Clermont," the first steamer that ever navigated American waters. She soon made regular trips between New York and Albany, and although her rate of speed at first was only five miles an hour, this was soon increased by improved machinery. The darling object of his life was accomplished; steam navigation was now no vague theory, but an established fact, and from that time (1807) steamboats were multiplied on all the waters of the United States, from the St. Lawrence to the Gulf of Mexico. His success was now wafted on every breeze, and the penniless schoolboy of Lancaster county, Pennsylvania, wore a well-earned coronet of fame. He constructed, in 1807, a large boat named "The Car of Neptune," which plied the waters of the Hudson with increased speed, being a great improvement on the "Clermont." In 1809 Fulton obtained his first patent from the United States, and the usual penalty of excessive litigation incident to all prominent inventors absorbed the next two years of his eventful life. In 1811 he was appointed one of the commissioners to explore the route of an inland navigation from the Hudson river to the Lakes. He afterwards constructed ferry-boats to run between New York city and the New Jersey shore, a large boat for Long Island Sound, five for the Hudson, and several for the Ohio and Mississippi rivers. In 1814 Congress authorized the President to build one or more batteries for coast defence, and Fulton was appointed to superintend their construction. He commenced the construction of a war steamer and launched it within four months. It was called the "Demologos," afterwards named "Fulton the First." It was a heavy, unwieldy mass, and could only make about three miles an hour, but it was considered a marvel and a most potent engine of defence. In 1815 he attended the Legislature of New Jersey as a witness, and in crossing the Hudson on his return caught a severe cold, which terminated his life, February 24, 1815, at the comparatively early age of fifty. He was considered by his compeers and the general public as one of the rare men of the period. He possessed solid ability, tact, pluck, patience, and enthusiasm, and was one of the most popular men in the State of New York, his death there being recognized as a great public calamity. He died in the midst of his triumphs and in the height of his fame. In 1806 he married Harriet, the daughter of Walter Livingston, a relative of his life-long, steadfast friend, the Chancellor.

There was something intensely prepossessing in the personal appearance of Robert Fulton. His figure was slender, a little above the ordinary size, and his large, dark eyes and features of manly beauty rendered him an exceedingly handsome man. His conversational powers were vivacious and sparkling, and he possessed the manners and address of a natural gentleman. In 1846 Congress passed an act appropriating $76,200 in full of the claim of Fulton against the United States for inventing floating steam batteries, and applying steam to navigation— a worthy recognition of the services of a distinguished man of whom Pennsylvania and the country may well feel proud.

APPENDIX.

APPENDIX.

LIST OF GOVERNORS OF THE COLONIES ON THE DELAWARE, AND OF THE PROVINCE AND STATE OF PENNSYLVANIA, 1623–1876.

ACCESS.		EXIT.
1623	The Dutch planted a Colony on the Delaware, under Cornelius Jacob May, appointed Governor by the West India Company, under authority of the States General.	
1624	William Useling, appointed Governor of the Swedish Colony to be established on the Delaware. (Never arrived).	
1630	David Petersen DeVries (Dutch).	
1631	John Printz (Swedish).	
1638	Peter Minuit (Swedish, but himself a native of Holland)......................................	1640
1640	William Nieft, Dutch Governor of New York.	
1643	John Printz (Swedish).........................	1653
1653	John Papegoia (son-in-law of Printz)	1654
1654	John Claudius Risingh........................	1655
1655	Deryk Smidt (temporary)†.....................	1657
1655	Nov. 29th, John Paul Jaquet*..........	1657
1657	Jacob Alrich.................................	1659
1659	Alex. De Hinoyossa*..........................	1664

* Under Stuyvesant, Dutch Governor of New York.
† Colony divided into City and Company.

GOVERNORS UNDER THE CONSTITUTION OF THE STATE.

Two Pennsylvanians, both Revolutionary soldiers, were Presidents of the Continental Congress, viz., Gen. Thomas Mifflin, December, 1783, and Gen. Arthur St. Clair, February, 1787.

CHRONOLOGICAL HISTORY OF PENN-SYLVANIA, 1609–1776.

1609 Delaware Bay discovered by Captain Henry Hudson.

1616 The Delaware river explored as far as the Schuylkill, by Captain Hendrickson, in the yacht " Restless."

1618 Captain May gives his name to the Cape.

1623 Dutch settle on the shores of the Delaware.

1626 Dutch build a trading-house on Bile's Island, Bucks county.

1630 Dutch settle at Cape May.

1631 Captain DeVries arrived in the Delaware with two ships and colonists.

1635 War between the Leuni Lennappi and the Susquehannocks.

1638 Swedes arrived, and erected Fort Christina near the site of Wilmington.

1641 Minnit, the first Swedish Governor, died.

1642 Lutheran catechism translated into the Indian language by Campanius. Swedes laid the foundation of a capitol at Tinicum.

1646 Church erected at Tinicum. First mention of Upland, now Chester.

1648 Grant to Sir Edmund Ployden, as Governor and Earl Palatine.

1651 The Dutch erect Fort Casimer.

1655 Swedes on the Delaware subjugated by the Dutch, under Peter Stuyvesant.

1657 The name of Fort Christina changed to Altona, and that of Fort Casimer to New Amstel, now New Castle.

1664 New Netherlands conquered by the English, under Sir Robert Carr.

1672 Dutch recovered New Netherlands.

1673 George Fox, founder of the Quaker Society, visited the Colonies.

1675 Quakers settled at Upland.

1679 First vessel launched on Lake Erie. First English child born in Pennsylvania.

1681 William Penn received the charter of Pennsylvania, March 4th, on condition of yielding two beaver-skins annually.

1682 Penn arrived at New Castle, October 27th. Visited Upland, October 28th, and changed its name to Chester. Treaty of Amity under the Elm at Shackamaxon, November 4th. First session of Council and Assembly at Chester, December 4th. First Grand Jury of Pennsylvania summoned to attend Chester courts. First English child born in Philadelphia.

1683 First session of Council and Assembly held in Philadelphia, March 10th. Meetings for worship commenced at Darby, by Friends. Germantown founded. First Post-Office established in Philadelphia by William Penn. First sheriff of Philadelphia elected. Number of dwellings in Philadelphia, eighty.

1684 Pennsburg Manor-house, Bucks county, erected for William Penn. Population of Pennsylvania, 7,000; population of Philadelphia, 2,500.

1685 First book printed in the Middle Colonies by William Bradford, at Philadelphia. Court-house at Chester erected.

1688 Protest against slavery by the German Friends of Germantown.

1692 The Province taken from Penn. First school established at Darby.

1694 Penn's rights restored, August 30.

1695 Christ Church, Philadelphia, originally founded.

1697 Paper mill built by Bradford and the Rittenhuysens on the Wissahickon.

1698 Shawnees Indians from Carolina settled on the Susquehanna. First Baptist and Presbyterian congregation formed in Philadelphia.

1699 Yellow fever raged in the Province. James Logan came to Pennsylvania.

1701 Penn's second visit to the Province, August, 1699. He remained till November, 1701. Philadelphia chartered as a city. Edward Shippen elected first Mayor of Philadelphia, under the charter. Penn returned to England.

1703 Separation of the three lower counties. Governor Andrew Hamilton died, April 20.

1704 First Presbyterian Church in Pennsylvania erected in Philadelphia, known as the "Old Buttonwood Church."

1705 An act passed to prevent the importation of Indians as slaves.

1710 French Huguenots settle on Pequea Creek, Lancaster county.

1712 William Penn seized with paralysis. An act passed forbidding the importation of negroes as slaves.

1714 Conrad Weiser came to this country from Germany.

1715 Governor Gookin held a council with the Indians at Philadelphia. First regularly organized Baptist Church in Delaware county.

1718 William Penn died at Ruscombe, England, July 30th, at the age of 74 years. Dunkers settled about Germantown and in Lancaster county. Hannah Penn for some time exercises the proprietor's prerogatives, through representatives.

1720 First Iron Furnaces erected in Pennsylvania.

1721 First Insurance Office opened in Philadelphia.

1722 Irish and Scotch settlements made in Donegal and Paxton.

1723 Benjamin Franklin arrived in Philadelphia. Paper money first issued in the Province. Act passed reducing the rate of interest from eight to six per cent.

1726 "Log College," on Neshaminy creek, Bucks county, established by Rev. William Tennant. First Iron Works erected in Lancaster county.

1727 First German Reformed ministers arrived in Pennsylvania.

1728 The Carpenter's Society established, 1724; Bartram's Botanic Garden, near Gray's Ferry, commenced.

1729 First mill built, near the site of Mercersburg, Franklin county. First permanent settlement in York county. Work commenced on the old State-house, Philadelphia; completed 1734. Temporary Court-house and Jail built near Lancaster. Duty laid on foreigners and Irish servants imported into the Province.

1730 Thomas Godfrey invented the Quadrant.

1731 The Library Company, of Philadelphia, founded. First Baptist church erected in Philadelphia. Inoculation first practiced in Pennsylvania.

1732 Dunkers settled at Ephrata, Lancaster county.

1733 First German Reformed church erected at Germantown. First negroes emancipated in Pennsylvania. First Roman Catholic church erected in Philadelphia. First Lutheran church erected in the Province. First classical school erected at Ephrata.

1734 First Episcopal church in Lancaster county, erected at Conestoga. Silk, in small quantities, manufactured in the Province. First Masonic lodge in Pennsylvania organized in Philadelphia, Benjamin Franklin, Master.

17.5 John Penn resides in the Province from 1734 to 1735; Thomas Penn from 1732 to 1741.

1736 Governor Gordon died in August.

1737 Benjamin Franklin appointed Postmaster of Philadelphia.

1738 Conrad Weiser and William Parsons visit Wyoming. Benjamin West, the great American artist, born in Springfield township, Delaware county, October 10. First Presbyterian church erected near the site of Mercersburg. First fire company organized in Philadelphia.

1739 Rev. George Whitfield arrived. Moravian settlement commenced at the Forks of the Delaware.

1740 War declared against France. First Sabbath-school in America established at Ephrata. Lazaretto erected for sick immigrants at Tinicum, on the Delaware river. First permanent settlement at Bethlehem.

1741 York laid out. Whitfield's church, Fourth street, Philadelphia, erected. Count Zindendorf arrived in the Province.

1742 Rev. Henry M. Muhlenberg arrived. German Reformed minister at Germantown ordained by Bishop

Nitschman. Election riot in Philadelphia, October 1. Treaty with the Six Nations at Philadelphia.

1743 First German Lutheran church in Philadelphia, St. Michael's, erected. Sister's house at Bethlehem erected. American Philosophical Society organized in Philadelphia; incorporated 1780; building erected 1785.

1744 Proclamation of war against France made in Philadelphia in June.

1745 General Anthony Wayne born in Chester county. Lindley Murray, Grammarian, born in Lancaster county. Franklin stoves invented by Dr. Franklin.

1747 First Steel furnace erected in Philadelphia by Stephen Paschall.

1748 First Public Lottery sanctioned by the Legislature. Fort de la Presque Isle erected.

1749 Lewis Evans published a map of the Middle Colonies, An Academy and Charitable school established in Philadelphia. It 1750 it was opened as a Latin school; in 1753 it was incorporated and endowed; in 1755 it was chartered under the title of "The College Academy and Charitable School of Philadelphia;" and in 1799 it became the University of Pennsylvania. First settlement in Tuscarora valley made by Scotch-Irish.

1751 Pennsylvania Hospital at Philadelphia founded buildings erected, 1755 to 1804. The Loganian Library founded.

1752 First Fire Insurance Company in the Colonies, "The Philadelphia Contributionship," established. Franklin and Kinnersley establish the identity of electricity and lightning. State-house bell imported from England; re-cast in Philadelphia, 1873.

1753 Washington's expedition to Venango; the Forks of the Ohio fortified by his advice; he visits the Half King Tarracharison, and the Queen Alliquippa. Franklin appointed Deputy Postmaster-General for the British Colonies. French invaded Western Pennsylvania. Beginning of the French and Indian war.

1754 First settlement on the site of Pittsburgh. Fort Du Quesne built by the French. March of Colonial troops for the Ohio country, April 22. Battle of Great Meadows, May 28. Washington in command of the troops, May 30. Surrender of Fort Necessity, July 4.

1755 Defeat of Braddock, July 9. Braddock died of wounds, July 13.

1756 England declared war against France, May 17. Fort Granville, on the Juniata, burned by Indians, July 30. Fort Halifax, Dauphin county, erected. Kittanning destroyed by Colonel Armstrong, September 8. First line of stages and wagons between Philadelphia and Baltimore.

1757 First Weekly Post between Philadelphia and Carlisle.

1758 The French retreat from Fort Du Quesne, November 24.

1759 First Theatre erected in Philadelphia. Company for Insurance on Lives (Presbyterian) established.

1760 Products of Pennsylvania so vast as to require 8,000 to 9,000 wagons for transportation to Philadelphia. Classical school established in Cumberland Valley.

1862 Connecticut settlers arrived at Wyoming, and are attacked by Indians. War with Spain declared. George III. proclaimed in Pennsylvania, January 21.

1763 Peace concluded at Paris, February 10. Pontiac's war. Mason and Dixon commenced running boundary line between Pennsylvania and Maryland. Massacre of settlers in Wyoming county by Indians, October 15.

1764 Colonel Henry Boquet's expedition against the Indians. Medical department of the University of Pennsylvania founded—the oldest medical school in the country.

1765 Stamp Act passed, March 8. Robert Fulton born in Lancaster county.

1766 Stamp Act repealed, March 18.

1769 Methodism first introduced into Pennsylvania. American Philosophical Society founded.

1773 First Methodist Conference in the United States held in Philadelphia. First Steamboat floated on the

11

Schuylkill by Oliver Evans. Resolutions passed in the Province to resist the duty on Tea, October 18.

1774 First Continental Congress assembled in Carpenter's Hall, Philadelphia, September 5. Resolutions against the Slave Trade passed by the First Congress.

1775 Second Continental Congress assembled in Philadelphia, May 10. First Pennsylvania company that marched to the seat of war was a company of riflemen from York, July 1. Continental money first issued.

1776 Declaration of Independence adopted, July 4. Read from the rear of the State-house, July 8. Convention for forming State Constitution met in Philadelphia, July 15. Declaration of Independence signed, August 2. Washington retreated across the Delaware, December 8.

1777 Battle of Brandywine, September 11. Congress adjourned to Lancaster, September 18. Massacre at Paoli, September 20. British occupied Philadelphia, September 26. Congress assembled at Lancaster and adjourned to York, September 27. Supreme Executive Council met at Lancaster, October 1. Battle of Germantown, October 4. British fleet sailed up the Delaware, November 18. Washington retired to Valley Forge, December 11.

1778 British evacuated Philadelphia, June 18. Battle of the Kegs, January 7. Battle of Wyoming, July 3 and 4.

1782 Preliminary Treaty of Peace signed at Paris, November 30.

1783 Cessation of hostilities proclaimed, April 19. Treaty of Peace signed at Paris, September 3. Continental Army disbanded, November 3.

1786 An Act passed appropriating the proceeds of 60,000 acres of land in aid of Public Schools, April 7.

1787 Convention for framing the National Constitution met in Philadelphia, May 10. Continued in session until September 17. National Constitution adopted, September 17.

1789 " Pennsylvania Society for Promoting the Abolition of Slavery " incorporated. Convention for framing the new State Constitution met in Philadelphia, November 24.

1791 First " Bank of the United States " incorporated, February 25.

1793 Washington's second inauguration took place in old Congress Hall, March 4. Wayne's campaign, 1793 to 1795.

1796 First Type Foundry in America established in Philadelphia. General Anthony Wayne died at Presque Island, September 27.

1797 John Adams inaugurated President, March 4.

1799 State Legislature met in Lancaster.

1800 Seat of the Federal Government removed from Philadelphia to Washington, D. C.

1802 An Act passed for the education of the poor, gratis.

1804 The frigate Philadelphia gallantly burned by Decatur, in the harbor of Tripoli.

1806 First Railroad in the United States built in Ridley township, Delaware county.

1811 First steamboat launched at Pittsburgh.

1812 Legislature removed to Harrisburg. Steam waterworks at Fairmount commenced. Declaration of war against Great Britain, June 19.

1813 Perry's fleet built in Erie in seventy days; his victory, September 10. The American Flotilla under Lieutenant Angus, engage the British vessel Junon, 38 guns, and Martin, 16 guns, outside Crows' Shoals, July 29.

1814 Battle of Fort Erie, August 15. Sortie at Fort Erie, September 17.

1816 Pittsburgh incorporated as a city. Second " Bank of the United States," at Philadelphia, chartered April 10.

1818 First Light-house on the Great Lakes erected at Presque Isle; rebuilt, 1857. Lehigh Canal commenced; completed 1838.

1819 Corner-stone of the State Capitol at Harrisburg laid, May 31; main building completed, 1821.

1820 General Synod of the Lutheran Church established.

1822 State Legislature first met in the State Capitol at Harrisburg.

1824 Lafayette's second visit to Pennsylvania. American Sunday-school Union formed in Philadelphia.

1825 Schuylkill Navigation Canal completed; commenced 1815. Historical Society of Pennsylvania established.

1827 Paper made from straw at Meadville, by Col. William Magraw.

1834 Common school system of Pennsylvania established, May 1. Railroad and Canal opened to Pittsburgh. First Homeopathic Medical school in the world erected at Allentown.

1838 Convention to revise State Constitution met at Philadelphia, and closed their labors, February 22. The amended Constitution adopted by the people at the next election. Buckshot war, December 4–8.

1839 The Pennsylvania banks suspended specie payments, August 13.

1844 " Native American " and Irish riot in Philadelphia; 30 houses and 3 churches burned ; 14 persons killed, and 40 wounded.

1846 First Telegraph lines erected in Pennsylvania.

1851 Christiana riot, Lancaster county, against the attempt to rescue fugitive slaves, September 11.

1854 Normal School at Philadelphia founded.

1857 Normal School Act passed.

1859 Agricultural College of Pennsylvania, Centre county, opened. Success of Col. Drake in boring for Petroleum, August 29.

1860 People of Pittsburgh refused to permit the shipment of ordnance from the Arsenal to Southern forts, December 24.

1861 Act passed to organize the Militia of the State, April 12. Bill passed by the State Senate to define and punish treason, April 13. Two Pennsylvania regiments raised for the United States reported ready for service, April 13. Five companies of Pennsylvania volunteers, accompanied by regular troops from Carlisle, reached Washington, D. C., April 18, being the first volunteer troops that entered the National Capital, under the call of President Lincoln. Act passed to organize the Reserve Corps of the Commonwealth, May 15. Lieutenant John T. Greble, of Philadelphia, killed at the battle of Great Bethel, Va., June 10, the first Pennsylvania officer who fell in the war for the Union. Pennsylvania Reserve Corps marched to the defence of Washington, July 21.

1862 The whole Militia force of the State called out by Governor Curtin, September 14, to repel invasion of the State. General Stuart's Confederate cavalry made a raid into Pennsylvania, demanded the surrender of Chambersburg, destroyed the military stores, burned the machine-shops, depot buildings, etc., October 10.

1863 Second invasion of Pennsylvania. Lee advances north of Chambersburg, June 16. Confederates occupied the town. Skirmish near Gettysburg, June 23. Confederates advanced to Shippensburg, June 24; near Carlisle, June 25. Confederates occupied Gettysburg, and Unionists evacuated Carlisle, June 26. General Meade assumed command of the Army of the Potomac; Confederates occupied York; threatened Harrisburg; skirmish at Columbia Bridge; bridge burned, June 28. Confederates shelled Carlisle on the night of July 1. Battle of Gettysburg, July 1-3. General Reynolds killed, July 1.

1864 Great Sanitary Fair at Logan Square, Philadelphia, opened June 7. Third invasion of Pennsylvania by the Confederates, July. Chambersburg burned, July 30.

1868 Corner-stone of the new Masonic Temple in Philadelphia laid June 24. James Buchanan, ex-President of the United States, died at Wheatland, near Lancaster, June 1. Thaddeus Stevens died at Washington, D. C., August 11; buried at Lancaster.

1873 Convention to revise State Constitution met in Philadelphia, and closed their labors, November 3. Constitution adopted, December 16, 1873.

1876 Centennial of the Independence of the States; International Exposition at Philadelphia, July 4.

TABULAR STATEMENT OF TROOPS FUR-NISHED BY PENNSYLVANIA DURING THE REBELLION.

1861.

Under call of the President, April 15th, 1861,
for three months........................... 20,979

" Pennsylvania Reserve Volunteer corps," originally intended for State service, but sent
into the service of the General Government,
under call of the President, of July 22, 1861,
for three years............................. 15,856

Organized under Act of Congress of July 22,
1861, for three years....................... 93,759
————— 130,594

1862.

Under the call of the President of July 7th, 1862,
including 18 nine month regiments.......... 40,383

Organized under draft of August 4th, 1862, for
nine months................................ 15,100

Independent companies for three years....... 1,358

Recruits forwarded by Superintendents of Recruiting Service............................ 9,250

Enlistments in other State organizations, and
in the Regular Army....................... 5,000
————— 71,100

1863.

Organized under special authority of War Department, for three years.................. 1,066

Under call of the President, June, 1863:

For six months............................ 4,484

For emergency............................ 7,062

Recruits forwarded by Superintendents of Recruiting Service............................ 4,458

Enlistments in Regular Army............... 934

Ninety days militia, June, 1863.............. 25,042
————— 43,046

1864.

Re-enlistment in old organizations, for three
  years...................................... 17,876
Organized under special authority from War
  Department, for three years................ 9,867
Under call July 27th, for one year........... 16,094
Under call July 6th, for one hundred days... 7,675
Recruits forwarded by Superintendents of Re-
  cruiting Service........................... 26,567
Drafted men and substitutes................. 10,651
Recruits for Regular Army..... 2,974
                                                     ———— 91,704

1865.

(Recruiting for volunteers, ceased in April of
  this year),
Under call of the President, of December 19th,
  1864, for one year.................. 9,645
Recruits forwarded by Superintendents of Re-
  cruiting Service........................... 9,133
Drafted men and substitutes................. 6,675
Recruits for Regular Army............ 387
                                                     ———— 25,840

Total number of men furnished..........   . 362,284

The above statement does not include the 25,000 Militia in
active service in September 1862.

CONTENTS.